CHRISTOPHER
WALKEN
A TO Z

CHRISTOPHER
WALKEN

A TO Z

THE MAN · THE MOVIES · THE LEGEND

BY ROBERT SCHNAKENBERG

QUIRK BOOKS
PHILADELPHIA

Library of Congress Cataloging in Publication Number: 2008922978

ISBN: 978-1-59474-259-0

Designed by Doogie Horner

Printed in China
Typeset in Bembo and Trade Gothic
Photos courtesy of the Everett Collection

Distributed in North America by Chronicle Books
680 Second Street
San Francisco, CA   94107

10 9 8 7 6 5 4 3 2

Quirk Books
215 Church Street
Philadelphia, PA   19106
www.quirkbooks.com

"I am a foreigner in my own country because I come from another country, the country of show business."

—Christopher Walken

INTRODUCTION

"The one advantage that I have," Christopher Walken once observed, "is that if you're looking for a Chris Walken type, you have got to get Chris Walken."

It's true. No other actor embodies the term "one of a kind" quite so fully as Walken. The ageless wonder from Astoria, Queens is *sui generis*—a self-made cinematic icon whose appeal transcends generations and whose unique persona enlivens whatever genre in which he happens to be working. He's been called the prince of pallor, the duke of spook. He's been a Broadway chorus boy, a dramatic leading man, and the hardest-working character actor in show business. He's played sexy gigolos, power-hungry megalomaniacs, doting fathers, and many, many ruthless gangsters. He even played a singing, dancing cat in a movie adaptation of *Puss in Boots*. Fittingly, given his idiosyncratic tastes, it's one of his favorite roles.

Born Ronald Walken in 1943 to German and Scottish immigrants, Walken worked in his parents' bakery and eventually joined his two brothers on the child acting circuit. He parlayed that experience into a career in musical theater in the 1960s, made the transition to the dramatic stage, and appeared in Hollywood films beginning in the early 1970s. His Academy Award-winning performance in *The Deer Hunter* in 1978 catapulted him onto the A-list, where he has remained (with occasional forays into B movies) ever since. That rare performer who combines celebrity cachet with indie street cred,

Walken is also one of the most imitated actors this side of William Shatner—thanks to his incredibly odd speaking pattern.

Through it all, Christopher Walken has not lost his ability to shock, surprise, and defy expectations. Audiences are constantly rediscovering him. "Who knew he could dance?" some said when they first saw him do so in *Pennies from Heaven* in 1981, or the video for Fatboy Slim's "Weapon of Choice" in 2000, or in *Hairspray* in 2007. Others are amazed to learn this two-time Oscar nominee once worked as a lion tamer, had a cable TV cooking show, and used to worship the moon. After all, as Walken himself once wrote—in a play about a transvestite Elvis Presley—"If you can't surprise yourself, you can't surprise anyone else."

With so many unexpected twists and turns, the time seemed right for a guidebook to Walkenland. As you leaf through these pages, you will get a sense of the man—his passions, predilections, and personal quirks. You will also have a handy portable cheat sheet as you continue your Walken studies. A star rating guide to every movie in the Walken canon will help you sort through the dreck to find the really essential Walken performances. Wherever possible, Walken's own words—compiled from the hundreds of interviews he's given over the years—are reprinted in context to allow his own original personality to shine through. Feel free to read them aloud in your best Christopher Walken voice to achieve the full effect.

Christopher Walken may feel like a foreigner in his own country, but you'll emerge from this book feeling like a native inhabitant of his strange and unique world.

WALKEN SURVEYS HIS NATIVE CITY IN ABEL FERRARA'S *KING OF NEW YORK*.

A NOTE ABOUT
THE ENTRIES

Items in bold face are cross-references to other entries in *Christopher Walken A to Z*.

A four-star rating system has been provided to help you prioritize your Walken consumption. Each of his films has been rated as follows.

★★★★	Prime grade, essential Walken. The *ice* is gonna *break* if you don't see this!
★★★	Rent it. This movie is as good as it's gonna get—and it won't ever get that good again.
★★	Feel free to skip this one. Needs more Walken!
★	Awful. You get ten years in a cell with a psycho gorilla for even thinking of watching this.

A to B

ABBOTT, JACK HENRY

Walken attended the January 1982 murder trial of career criminal and literary cause célèbre Jack Henry Abbott in New York City. Charged in the stabbing death of a Manhattan waiter, Abbott was found guilty and sentenced to fifteen years to life in prison. He hanged himself in his cell in March 2002.

Abbott's case attracted the attention of author Norman Mailer, who championed Abbott's burgeoning literary career and tried to get his epistolary jailhouse memoir *In the Belly of the Beast* adapted for the big screen. Walken was briefly under consideration for the role of Abbott, which may explain his presence at the trial. "I often go to court to watch people's emotions," the actor explained to a reporter for the *New York Post* as he exited the courtroom. Public interest in Abbott receded after his murder conviction, and the film was never made.

Oddly enough, despite ample photographic evidence to the contrary, in subsequent interviews Walken has denied ever having attended Abbott's trial. "I asked Mailer if he could get me into the courtroom because I wanted to take a look at the guy," he told interviewers in 1988. "He said no. But I must say that I was so turned off that I never followed up on it."

ACTORS STUDIO

For fifteen years, Walken worked as a janitor at this legendary New York City studio, best known as the birthplace of American method acting. Although not a practitioner of "The Method" himself, Walken took the opportunity—when he wasn't building sets, replacing light bulbs, or doing other handiwork—to attend acting classes moderated by Elia Kazan, Ellen Burstyn, Al Pacino, and, of course, venerable acting teacher Lee Strasberg. "I found [Strasberg] rather severe," Walken later recalled. "He had humor, but you rarely saw it. Elia Kazan was the best acting teacher I ever saw. He says such simple things." By contrast, Walken found some of his colleagues and mentors at the Studio full of self-importance. "There were these people who'd [act like] some kind of Delphic mysteries were being imparted," he has said. "Such seriousness. I said to somebody once, 'Please, I'm getting a headache.' She said to me, 'You just don't understand.' I haven't been there in ten years for that reason."

Despite his reservations, Walken finally auditioned for and won admittance to the Studio in the late 1970s. His most memorable lesson, which he has recounted in numerous interviews over the years, came by way of Strasberg. Walken was performing a scene from *Death of a Salesman* at the Studio when someone off-stage dropped a large box of dishes. The loud noise distracted the audience and the other actors, but not Walken, who went right on playing the scene. Afterwards Strasberg asked him about the incident. "Everyone jumped except you," Strasberg said. You didn't even react." "Yes," Walken replied. "I was concentrating." "That's not concentrating," Strasberg countered, "that's bad acting." "That was a big moment for me," Walken later recalled. "I realized that concentration isn't about focusing. It's about having 360-degree vision, eyes and ears open, not missing a thing."

ADDICTION, THE ★★★

Walken has a memorable cameo as a jaded New York vampire who's learned to curtail his bloodlust through mental discipline in this superb revisionist horror movie from director **Abel Ferrara**. Lili Taylor stars as Kathleen Conklin, an NYU grad student who has the bite put on her late one night by a punked-out Annabella Sciorra. Taylor spends the next eighty minutes turning every person she meets into a desiccated, heliophobic bloodsucker like herself. She also finds the time to complete her PhD dissertation, which is quite an accomplishment considering half the faculty is now made up of vampires. There's much analogizing of vampirism to **drug** addiction, and some half-baked philosophy thrown in (*de rigeur* in a Ferrara movie), but the real draw here is Walken. In his second film for Ferrara and screenwriter Nicholas St. John, Walken plays Peina, a hipster cross between Dracula and Colonel Kurtz from *Apocalypse Now*. "You wanna go someplace dark?" he says to Lili Taylor when they first meet. Soon he's regaling her with quotations from *Naked Lunch* and his own personal prescription for keeping your plasma jones in check. He also takes a moment to suck her blood. It's a weirdly mesmeric performance in a weirdly mesmeric film. For the record, *The Addiction* also boasts one of the all-time great horror movie climaxes, as a staid philosophy department party becomes the setting for a grisly vampire orgy. Bloody good fun for viewers of all ages.

> *"The entire world's a graveyard and we, the birds of prey picking at the bones."*
>
> —Peina, dishing out some chicken soup for the vampire soul, in 1995's *The Addiction*

AFFAIR OF THE NECKLACE, THE ★★

Eighteenth century France provides the setting for Walken to portray yet another debauched European (see *The Comfort of Strangers* and *Illuminata* for other examples). This time he dons a funky mullet wig and a Van Dyke beard that makes him look like the guy dressed up as Satan at a Halloween party. As Count Alessandro di Cagliostro, "grandmaster of the Illuminati, accomplished alchemist and mesmerist," he brings a delicious air of menace to this otherwise tedious 2001 costume drama, which recreates the real-life events in an infamous scandal that brought the monarchy into disrepute around the time of the French Revolution. Hilary Swank and Simon Baker are the romantic leads, with Walken's old *A Business Affair* sparring part-

PLAYING A DISSOLUTE ITALIAN NOBLEMAN, WALKEN CHEWS
THE SCENERY IN 2001'S *THE AFFAIR OF THE NECKLACE*.

ner Jonathan Pryce on hand as a scheming cardinal (is there any other
kind in a Hollywood film?).

AFTERLIFE
"Life is so amazing to me that I find it hard to believe it stops,"
Walken has observed. His belief in a world beyond this one originated in **childhood**, when he was overcome by the senselessness of
death while attending the funeral of his beloved uncle. Standing in
front of the open casket, Walken experienced a kind of existential

epiphany. "Everybody was tearing their hair out. And I remember thinking, 'This is impossible, I don't believe it. It can't be that you're just dead.' And I still feel that way." Declaring flatly that "I don't believe in death," Walken also contends that there is a special type of immortality reserved for actors. "The other night I was watching a movie on TV and there was an actor in it I really like. Then it crossed my mind that he's dead. But he's not dead; there he is, you know?"

ALI, MUHAMMAD

The former heavyweight champion and self-styled "greatest of all time" is one of Walken's heroes. In the early 1970s, Walken kept a framed, autographed pair of Ali's soiled white boxing trunks on the wall in his New York apartment. Walken was also one of the few moviegoers to come away with a favorable impression of Ali's portrayal of himself in the critically derided 1977 biopic *The Greatest*. "I was really impressed with his performance," Walken told an interviewer shortly after seeing the picture. "It was a silly film, but to see him in front of a camera was incredible. He was light, he was funny, and he handled women with such charm—almost like Cary Grant. He's got it."

ALL-AMERICAN MURDER ★

If you consider the words "A Film by Anson Williams" a mark of quality in the opening credits of a movie, then by all means rent this 1992 straight-to-video shocker directed by the man who played Potsie on *Happy Days*. It's unfathomable why Walken chose to lend his prestige to this preposterous thriller, which stars Charlie Schlatter (of the short-lived sitcom *Ferris Bueller*) as a pyromaniacal college student wrongfully accused of the murder of a popular coed. Walken plays Detective P. J. "Deck" Decker, the hard-bitten homicide cop assigned to the case. He spends most of his time ruminating on the declining state of police work and issuing statements like: "I had a mission once. There were good guys and bad guys. Now it's a toilet. We separate the turds." He might have applied that logic when reading the script for this cinematic stinkbomb. Walken's made his share of bad movies, but never have his talents seemed so mismatched with the material. Performing alongside such comparative Lilliputians as Schlatter and Richard Kind, he seems to have beamed in from an entirely different movie. Gory, badly acted, and unpleasant from start to finish, *All-American Murder* may not be the worst film of Walken's entire career (see *Gigli*, *Envy*, or *Kangaroo Jack* for that distinction), but it's easily the most forgettable—at least until *Kiss Toledo Goodbye* in 1998.

> *"I never forget a face—especially if I've sat on it."*
>
> —Detective P. J. Decker, trying out his hostage negotiation skills on an armed robber, in Anson Williams' *All-American Murder*

AMERICA'S SWEETHEARTS   ★★

Walken plays a maniacal movie director who lives in the Unabomber's old cabin in this 2001 comedy written by funnyman Billy Crystal. Crystal plays a studio publicist trying to keep the peace between two feuding, divorced costars (John Cusack and Catherine Zeta-Jones) at a press junket for Walken's latest movie, which Crystal won't allow anyone to see. As Hal Weidmann, a Hollywood maverick reportedly based on Hal Ashby, Walken dons long gray hair extensions and flared jeans, and channels his inner auteur. He looks more like a deranged Vietnam veteran than a cinematic genius, but if you play along his scenes are mildly amusing. The rest of the film isn't nearly as good. The attempts at movie industry satire fall flat, while the two-dimensional lead characters—not to mention a couple of egregious ethnic caricatures from

WALKEN PLAYS A HOLLYWOOD BURN-OUT MODELLED ON
DIRECTOR HAL ASHBY IN *AMERICA'S SWEETHEARTS*.

Hank Azaria and Alan Arkin—doom this film from the start.

AMSTERDAM, MOREY

This mush-mouthed, Chicago-born comedian, best known for his
portrayal of comedy writer Buddy Sorrell on TV's *Dick Van Dyke
Show*, presided over Walken's graduation ceremony at the Professional
Children's School alongside burlesque legend **Gypsy Rose Lee**. In
keeping with PCS custom, both Amsterdam and Lee autographed
Walken's diploma.

ANAL PROBING

Inspired by his portrayal of anally-probed UFO abductee Whitley Streiber in the film *Communion*, Walken seems comfortable with the prospect that aliens would use this method of information extraction. "They have to do something," he says. "I like the idea that aliens would be benevolent. Why wouldn't they be?"

ANALYSIS

"I've thought a lot about going into analysis, because talking about myself is such a wonderful, enriching experience," Walken once observed. Yet he's also expressed a fear that resolving his neuroses would have an adverse effect on his art. "It would be like throwing money in the river for me to go into therapy. Why get rid of the things that are your friction, the film in your Brownie? I can't think of anything more tedious than an actor who's got himself straightened out. The only thing left for him to do is get a job with an insurance company."

Walken has confessed to submitting to one and only one round of analysis, at the suggestion of some friends in the late 1970s. But the therapist's messy apartment drove the notoriously tidy actor up the wall. "She had all these pots and pans and dishes piled everywhere," he later remembered. "I thought 'How am I going to take advice from someone like that?' That was the end of my shrinkage. Maybe if she had been clean and nice I'd still be in therapy."

See also **Cleanliness.**

ANDERSON TAPES, THE   ★★

Fourteen years before he worked with Roger Moore as **James Bond** in *A View to a Kill*, Walken shared the screen with the original 007, Sean Connery, in this 1971 caper movie from director Sidney Lumet. Walken plays "The Kid," an unnamed, long-haired electronics wizard who assists Connery in a scheme to burglarize a luxury apartment building in New York City. The film, which plays like *Ocean's Eleven* crossed with *The Taking of Pelham One Two Three*, was Connery's first big post-Bond role and Walken's major studio debut. (He receives an "Introducing" credit, although he'd previously appeared in the low-budget indie release *Me and My Brother* in 1969.) Dyan Cannon, Martin Balsam, and Alan King also appear.

The shoot left a lasting impression on the twenty-seven-year-old Walken. "It was a great kind of accident," he said many years later. "There I was with all these terrific actors." Sidney Lumet's method of rehearsal, which drew on Walken's experience as a stage performer, helped make the transition to screen acting a smooth one. "We went into a big room with tape on the floor, the way most plays are initially rehearsed, and we went through it scene by scene, just like a play. And then, when it came time to shoot it, it did make things a lot easier." It would be seventeen years before Walken collaborated on another Connery caper—starring opposite Sean's son Jason in the 1988 children's musical *Puss in Boots*.

> *"America, man, you know it's so beautiful,*
> *I want to eat it!"*
>
> —The Kid, expressing his love for the red, white, and blue in 1971's *The Anderson Tapes*

ANNIE HALL   ★★★★

"It could be I got the part in *The Deer Hunter* because of that," Walken has said of his brief but memorable appearance in Woody Allen's Oscar-winning 1977 comedy. As Duane Hall, the disturbed brother of Diane Keaton's title character who dreams of committing suicide by **driving** his car into oncoming traffic, Walken shows early evidence of his ability to leave an indelible mark on a film in just a couple of short scenes. In fact, he has since confessed that he never even read the entire script. "I didn't know what the rest of the movie was," he told *Premiere* magazine in 2004. "I saw the two scenes I was in."

The performance is also a harbinger of the comic roles he would begin playing in the late 1980s. Walken credits *Annie Hall* with defining the contours of his subsequent career. "Somebody said that's probably why I started getting all those strange characters—because that was one of the first things I did that was seen by a lot of people. And here I was playing a suicide case . . . I guess one job leads to another. The next movie I did was *The Deer Hunter*, and I shoot myself, so it's hard to get cheery parts after that."

Oddly enough, Walken's career-making scene was nearly cut from the finished film. It was reinserted only a week before editing was completed because, Woody Allen said later, "We were getting such good responses we started to put back one or two things that we liked." Walken was such an afterthought, in fact, that his name isn't even spelled correctly in the end credits. He's listed as "**Christopher Wlaken**."

> *"I was called into an office. Woody Allen sat there. I don't remember that he ever said anything. And then I was in his movie."*
>
> —Walken, describing his "audition" for the role of Duane in *Annie Hall*

TOO SEXY FOR THE WOODMAN

Walken fans clamoring for a Woody Allen reunion almost got their wish in 1987, when the actor signed on to appear in the director's gloomy melodrama *September*. Originally cast as Peter, the struggling writer who spurns the affections of his Vermont neighbor in favor of her married best friend, Walken was replaced by Sam Shepard, who was replaced by Sam Waterston when Allen reshot the entire film with new actors in several key roles. While conceding that Walken is "a truly great actor," Allen told interviewer Stig Bjorkman that he "just wasn't right for the part. I can't explain this exactly, correctly. He was a little too sexy, a little too—not macho, but manly in a sexy way." Not the worst reason to lose a part, by any stretch of the imagination.

ANTZ ★★

Speaking of Woody Allen, the Woodman supplies the voice of the nebbishy worker drone known as "Z" in this 1998 computer-animated feature from DreamWorks studios. The action takes place in a New York City ant colony whose orderly social structure is challenged by the ambitious, ruthless General Mandible (voice of Gene Hackman). In his first-ever voice-over performance, Walken plays Colonel Cutter, Mandible's principal henchman, who at first assists and later turns on his unscrupulous superior. Sylvester Stallone, Sharon Stone, and Jennifer Lopez also "star" in the mildly amusing cartoon, which competed with Disney/Pixar's *A Bug's Life* for the hearts and minds of ant-obsessed moviegoers in the fall of 1998.

"Time stands still for no ant."

—Colonel Cutter, dropping some ant wisdom on Gene Hackman's evil General Mandible, in 1998's *Antz*

ARIES

Walken's zodiacal sign is Aries the Ram. According to astrological lore, major archetypes linked to Aries include the Leader, the Enthusiast, the Pioneer, the Warrior, the Daredevil, and the Competitor.

AROUND THE BEND   ★★

Walken won the Best Actor Award at the Montreal World Film Festival for his performance in this heartfelt 2004 feature from writer/director Jordan Roberts. If you can get past the implausibility of Walken being Michael Caine's son (and the bland Josh Lucas being related to either of them), then you might derive some satisfaction from this three-handkerchief family drama. Walken plays Turner Lair, a burned-out convict who staggers back into the life of his son Jason (Lucas) thirty years after abandoning him. Caine is Henry, Turner's eccentric, cockney, archaeologist father, whose sudden death provides the impetus for a little intergenerational reconciliation. Before you can say "road trip," Turner and Jason are out on the highway in a dilapidated VW van, with Jason's young son in tow, scattering Grampa's ashes and sharing family secrets and copious bags of Kentucky Fried Chicken. (Caine's character's weird, unexplained predilection for KFC becomes a major plot point.) The American Southwest provides the backdrop for all the noshing and confessing. At the film's high point, Walken rocks out under a desert moon to Fleetwood Mac's "Hi Ho Silver."

Straddling the line between bathos and wacky road comedy, *Around the Bend* is partially redeemed by Walken's powerful performance in one of his increasingly rare lead roles. Building on the delinquent dad persona he established in **Catch Me If You Can**, he brings a volcanic intensity to his portrayal of a guilt-ridden 1960s **drug** casualty compelled to expiate the sins of his reckless youth. As is his custom when preparing for a role, Walken drew on parallels to his own past, keying in particular on Turner's back story as a rock musician: "I was in musical comedy when I was a kid. I used to go to rock concerts and **Studio 54**. I was there. I had been a part of that. I saw Woodstock when it came out. As a matter of fact, I used to go to Woodstock before Woodstock was famous. So, all that was quite familiar to me. The idea that he was a musician. That for him, things didn't work out . . . so he's had some bumpy times." To convey Turner's ill health as a result of kidney failure, Walken also lost a lot of weight for the film. "I figured, you know, he's on death's doorstep. So I did make an effort to be a little bit emaciated. I look pretty awful in the movie, basically. And I'm supposed to." Also looking awful is Michael Caine, who, though he's only ten years older than Walken in real life, convincingly plays his elderly, dying father with the help of some heavy-duty age makeup. Josh Lucas has the somewhat thankless task of keeping up with these two screen legends, and playing off their very different acting styles. According to Lucas, Walken wasn't even sure what the film was about, a byproduct of his customary refusal to read the entire script. "It's not important to him," Lucas told an interviewer, "because he doesn't want to know. He wants to discover it. He wants to be like, 'Wait a sec. Why'd you say that line?' And he'll say that to you. At a certain point, you're like, 'Didn't you read the fucking script?' And he'll say, 'No. I did not read the script, motherfucker.' And you're like, 'Damn. That's a really interesting idea.'"

"It was a good part. A big, juicy part. I do a lot of parts where I am in the movie a little bit. Here's a part that I'm in almost all of it."

—Walken, explaining the allure of his role as a deadbeat dad in 2004's *Around the Bend*

ASTAIRE, FRED

This silver screen legend is one of Walken's heroes. Some have likened Walken's bravura performance in the Fatboy Slim music video **"Weapon of Choice"** to Astaire's fleet-footed dancing in films like *Royal Wedding*. Astaire and Walken actually met once, at a party following the premiere of the 1981 musical *Pennies from Heaven*. Although Astaire detested the film, he and fellow hoofer Gene Kelly went out of their way to compliment Walken on his dancing.

See also **Dance**.

ASTORIA, NY

Walken's birthplace is a neighborhood in the New York City borough of Queens, just a short subway ride from the heart of Manhattan. Named for millionaire John Jacob Astor (who threw down money to develop the area), Astoria has always been an ethnically diverse neighborhood. It is home to the world's oldest beer garden and was Archie Bunker's stomping ground on TV's *All in the Family*. Other notable Astoria-born celebrities include Tony Bennett, Whitey Ford, Ethel Merman, and David Schwimmer. British actor Patrick McGoohan was also born there, as was Red Hot Chili Pepper guitarist John Frusciante.

ASTRONOMY

As a child, Walken was a member of an amateur astronomy club—an avocation that came in handy many years later when he rented a house in Los Angeles with a telescope inside it. "There was a house across the way where they made porn movies, a lot of girls running around in teddies," he remembers. "The permanent residents wanted to get them out, but to me it didn't matter. I had my telescope."

AT CLOSE RANGE   ★★★

Walken delivers one of his most mesmerizing performances in this noirish 1986 feature. As ruthless small-time crime boss Bradley Whitewood Sr., he all but steals the film from a then up-and-coming Sean Penn, playing his ne'er-do-well son, Brad Jr., whom he initiates

WALKEN'S SEARING PORTRAYAL OF A CAREER CRIMINAL IN *AT CLOSE RANGE*
REPRESENTS THE HIGH POINT OF HIS MID-1980s "MOUSTACHE PERIOD."

into the world of thievery, corruption, and murder. Outfitted in a skeevy false moustache and lit satanically throughout, Walken is at his most menacing here, in a role turned down by Robert De Niro, who found it "too dark." That darkness didn't frighten Walken, who slipped into his thuggish Brad Sr. persona like a well-worn pair of jeans. "I remember the first scene we shot where I take him [Sean Penn's character] to launder the money," Walken told *Film Comment*. "I did that in one take and the director said, 'Well, you sure know who he is' and I said 'Yeah, sure.' And it was like that really from the first day."

It was Penn's idea to cast Walken: "It just came over me how unpredictable it would be for me to have someone that surprising in the part," Penn remarked. To prepare for their roles, the two actors drove from New York to Tennessee (where the film was shot) in Penn's pickup truck. (See **Driving**.) As he usually does, Walken found the basis for his portrayal in his own experience. "I think he really enjoyed his work," he said of Brad Sr. "There was a real glee in stealing. And I kind of translated that to myself; when I have fun being an actor, it's a pleasure. . . . Bad as he was, he never bothered me. He was a bad guy who enjoyed life." For good measure, Walken modeled Brad Sr.'s honeysuckle southern accent on two of his idols, **Muhammad Ali** and **Elvis Presley**.

At Close Range climaxes with a harrowing scene in which Brad Jr. confronts his father in his kitchen with an automatic weapon. Walken's terror in the scene is all too real, thanks to some off-screen trickery from Sean Penn. "In the middle of the take, he ran off the set and I heard him say to the propman, 'Give me the other gun,'" Walken told *Playboy*. "When he came back I was concerned that this wasn't the gun he had left with. Who knows? He's acting like some crazy actor and pointing it at my face, and it really scared me. It was near my eye," Walken said. "The goal is always to break things up and make them more effective," says Penn, "and I guess this was just more dramatic because it was a gun . . . so the fear on his face is real fear." "I believe Chris allowed himself to not know," added director James Foley. "He certainly knew that he could stop and ask. He allowed himself to have a question without an answer . . . because Sean's wacko enough. The main thing is, Chris couldn't be positive—and he didn't want to be. That's the kind of emotional calculus he uses, while other actors are just doing arithmetic." Thankfully, the **gun** was empty, but the switcheroo was enough to induce an added note of panic in Walken's performance. He would later pull the exact same trick on Matthew Broderick on the set of *Biloxi Blues* in 1987.

> *"He was sort of the dark side of the moon of Elvis or something. Somebody called him Hillbilly Lucifer."*
>
> —Walken, describing the character of Bradley Whitewood Sr. in *At Close Range*

AUDITIONS

Walken is notoriously reluctant to audition for roles, and this aversion is rooted in his earliest experiences as an actor. "What I used to do was, I'd get the script and see who the character was—a spy, a lumberjack, whatever—then I'd try to dress the part for the audition, to give the impression that I was tough or funny or whatever the part seemed to call for. That was always a disaster. I would never get the job. If I learned anything it's not to do anything like that. Now if they want to look at me, I go in and let them look at me. Let them figure out their own reasons for why they'd want to hire me." That approach clearly cost him the part in at least one picture, director Mike Figgis' feature debut *Stormy Monday* in 1988. Interviewed several years later for a book about directors' first-time film experiences, Figgis reported being "terrified" by his initial encounter with Walken, who was up for the part eventually played by Tommy Lee

Jones. "He flew a long way in for the meeting and was completely stoned when he turned up," Figgis remembered. "Very timidly I said 'Have you had a chance to look at the script?' He said, 'Look, do you like my face?' I went 'Yes.' He said, 'That's good. Because if you don't like my face, fuck you. Get De Niro. I'm out of here.' And he stood up and walked out of the room."

AUSTIN POWERS: INTERNATIONAL MAN OF MYSTERY

Reportedly, Walken was considered for the role of "Number Two" in the wildly popular 1997 comedy starring Mike Myers in the title role. The part of Dr. Evil's henchman eventually went to Walken's erstwhile boon companion, Robert "R. J." Wagner.

"BAD GIRL"

Walken plays Madonna's guardian angel—or is he the angel of death?—in this moody, stylized **music video** from future *Fight Club* director David Fincher. The Material Girl stars as Louise Oriole, a promiscuous, chainsmoking Manhattan career woman whose latest one-night stand may have murderous designs on her. Walken does a brief soft shoe routine but spends the majority of the five-minute film hovering in the background, glowering portentously, before planting the kiss of death on Her Madgesty in the video's eerie climax. Together they travel by crane, presumably to Heaven—or will it be The Other Place? Walken would move up to the lead role in his next music video, 2001's **"Weapon of Choice."**

BAKER STREET

Outfitted in alabaster stage makeup and an albino wig, Walken played a homicidal zombie in this 1965 Broadway **musical** adaptation of *The Adventures of Sherlock Holmes*. Veteran character actor

Fritz Weaver played the ingenious consulting detective, with future *Benson* regular Inga Svenson in the female lead. The unconventional take on Arthur Conan Doyle's sleuth garnered mixed reviews, but Walken (billed for the first time as **Christopher**) saw his villainous portrayal as something of a creative breakthrough. "I went around and shot and strangled," he told *Esquire* magazine in 1981. "At the end of the first act, I had this dance where I killed a guy. It was quite a good number, and I was aware for the first time of being able to move an audience around." Future Broadway fixture Tommy Tune played one of Walken's cohorts in crime.

    See also **Zombie Movies.**

BALLS OF FURY   ★★

Walken has had bad luck with lowbrow comedies in the first decade of the new millennium. *Envy*, *Joe Dirt*, and *Kangaroo Jack* all bombed, while *Click* and *The Wedding Crashers* largely wasted his talent in poorly developed supporting roles. *Balls of Fury* continues that unfortunate trend. This knuckledragger about a corpulent ping pong prodigy (Dan Fogler) who goes undercover for the FBI has a few laughs early on, but by the time Walken joins the action halfway through it's already spinning its wheels. He plays Master Feng, a mysterious mandarin madman who runs an underground table tennis tournament that's somehow, inexplicably, connected to a vast criminal enterprise. (Likewise, his utter lack of Chinese features and accent is never explained.) Adorned in silk robes and a **black** wig on loan from Ming the Merciless, Walken hams it up with gusto, although at times it seems as if he's reading his lines completely out of order. He puts the emphasis on words and syllables that seem totally unconnected to what he's talking about—even by Walkenesque standards. Around the set, many of Walken's remarks were equally cryptic. On the first day of shooting, Dan Fogler reports

AS MASTER FENG, WALKEN MONITORS THE PING-PONG
ACTION IN THE 2007 COMEDY *BALLS OF FURY.*

that Walken took him aside to share a little wisdom as they gazed out over Master Feng's koi pond. "Dan, you know what you, me, and the koi have in common?" Walken asked. "A billion heartbeats. No matter whether you're a gnat, you're the koi, you're a little dog, a munchkin—you got a billion heartbeats doled out to you by God."

"Less talky talky. More ping pong."

—Master Feng, perfectly encapsulating the lowbrow essence of 2007's *Balls of Fury*

BANANAS AND RICE

Foods Walken subsisted on for a week to achieve the haunted, hollowed-out look he wanted for the climactic scene in *The Deer Hunter*.

> *"In Thailand, they have thirty different kinds of bananas. I became a banana expert. And it did help me lose weight. I was very healthy, actually, in that section. I was probably in better shape than I've ever been in my life."*
>
> —Walken, on the benefits of his *"Deer Hunter* diet"

BAREFOOT IN ATHENS   ★★

Walken dons a toga as Lamprocles, the eldest son of Socrates, in this 1966 Hallmark Hall of Fame TV adaptation of Maxwell Anderson's historical play about the last days of the great Greek philosopher. Peter Ustinov plays Socrates in this static and stagy production, with Geraldine Page as his beloved wife, Xantippe. Walken has a few short scenes and gets to deliver one impassioned speech on his father's behalf during Socrates's trial. Evidently, television costume drama suited him well. He returned to the Hallmark Hall of Fame nine years later playing a Hessian major in an adaptation of another of Anderson's plays, *Valley Forge*.

BARRETT, RONA

This brassy gossip columnist and celebrity interviewer—born Rona Burstein—grew up two blocks away from Walken in **Astoria**, Queens.

BASQUIAT   ★★

Walken has a cameo as a vacuous journalist in his good friend Julian Schnabel's 1996 biopic about legendary downtown New York City graffiti artist Jean-Michel Basquiat. The cast is a veritable who's who of the New York acting scene in the 1990s—not to mention of gathering of erstwhile Walken costars. Benicio Del Toro, Dennis Hopper, Gary Oldman, Willem Dafoe, and Vincent Gallo have all appeared in other Walken projects. Walken's own part is small, but he effectively conveys the concentrated cluelessness of many of the art world interviewers of the period.

> *"How do you respond to being called the pickaninny of the art world?"*
>
> —The Interviewer, posing a typically insightful question to artist Jean-Michel Basquiat, in 1996's *Basquiat*.

BASTIANICH, LIDIA MATTICHIO

This respected restaurateur, chef, and host of TV **cooking** shows grew up across the street from the Walken family bakery in **Astoria, New York**. She worked part time for the Walkens throughout high school, first as a sales clerk and later as an assistant baker, cake decorator, and breadmaker. She credits her experience at the Walken bakery with inspiring her to pursue a culinary career.

See also **Food**.

BATMAN RETURNS   ★★★

Outfitted in an alabaster fright wig ("based on my **hair**" Walken insists) that makes him look like a deranged Thomas Jefferson, Walken played the sinister Gotham City industrialist Maximillian **"Max"** Shreck in this 1992 *Batman* sequel. The part represented a dream come true for Walken, who read Batman comics as a child. "In my house actually there was a room filled from floor to ceiling with comic books . . . My mother threw them away at some point. I must have had thousands."

A BEWIGGED WALKEN SURVEYS THE SHATTERED
LANDSCAPE OF GOTHAM CITY IN *BATMAN RETURNS*.

After taking on a number of dark, intense roles, playing Max also gave Walken an opportunity to return to a more overtly theatrical acting style "It's a costume movie," he told *Film Comment* magazine, "and doing it reminded me in certain ways of being in a play. My clothes were larger-than-life. . . . I don't usually do much physical transformation, so it was different in that way." Elsewhere he observed: "Max is absolutely out there. He makes no bones about his intentions. He's good to his family. He wears spats. I always wanted to wear spats."

Contrary to popular misconception, Walken did not base his characterization of Shreck on a certain brash New York real estate maven. "I never thought about Donald Trump," he told the *New York Times*. "I thought about the big show business moguls I read about. Sol Hurok. Sam Goldwyn. . . . And then I thought of a lawyer I know. An older guy. Real tough. Real New York. Real smart." He also thought of *The Great Gatsby*. Impressed by Shreck's resemblance to Meyer Wolfsheim, a gangster character in F. Scott Fitzgerald's novel who wears cuff links made out of human molars, Walken asked *Batman Returns* director Tim Burton to get him a pair of the toothy accessories. Within half an hour the prop man returned with them, which Walken proceeded to wear throughout the movie. "It's something the audience wouldn't know, but Burton knew it would be good for me to have them."

Molar cuff links aside, *Batman Returns* is widely considered the weak link in the original *Batman* movie cycle. Critics compared it unfavorably to its predecessor. Nevertheless, the film generated tremendous buzz and would prove to be an enormous worldwide hit. A glittering world premiere was staged at Mann's Chinese Theatre in Hollywood. Walken was the only person to show up in a tuxedo. Conceding that he got his notion of Hollywood premieres from old Hollywood movies, Walken confessed to feeling ridiculously overdressed. "There were a lot of motorcycle jackets. A lot of T-shirts. A lot of sporty clothes. I don't know. I felt like I was Robert Montgomery or somebody. At the party afterward, somebody came up to me and said, 'Gee, you sure look nice.' I felt like a jerk! In New York, I know what to do."

Max Shreck would prove to be one of Walken's most memorable cinematic creations. Years after *Batman Returns'* release, Walken was traveling with his wife in Italy when a local woman and her young son approached. As their paths crossed, the woman greeted him with a hearty "Buon giorno!" while the boy looked up at Walken and said "Max!"

"You're fired."

—Max Shreck, channeling the spirit of Donald Trump twelve years before *The Apprentice*, in 1992's *Batman Returns*

WALKEN'S MARCH OF THE PENGUINS

Besides providing him with an excuse to wear spats and molar cuff links, **Batman Returns** also gave Walken a rare opportunity to work with animals—specifically, the armies of flightless water fowl brought in to populate the Penguin's subterranean lair. During an appearance on *Late Night with David Letterman* to promote the film, Walken offered some random observations about his little waddling co-stars:

"I worked with the penguins every day. I got to like penguins very much and so did everybody else. Of course they were very well taken care of. They had trainers, they had people from the ASPCA watching."

"The penguins themselves, they're docile, very friendly, affectionate, like cats. There are two sizes. There's the big ones

YOUNG RONNIE WALKEN BUSTS A MOVE DURING
HIS EARLY DAYS AS A BROADWAY CHORUS BOY.

and the little ones. The big ones tend to eat a lot and then not eat for long time. The little ones are snappers, they like to eat all the time. And they come up to you and they hit you in the leg, you know, 'Feed me.'"

"There are a lot of real penguins [in the movie]—dozens— but there are also robot penguins which are controlled by people and also there are little people in penguin suits so not all the penguins are penguins."

"Toward the end they had another gig somewhere. . . . We were with them for a long time, weeks, and they had their own area, and a pool, and everything. And at some point we had to hurry up and get them done, because they had a gig in Europe."

BAYSIDE

As a child, Walken lived in this working-class Queens, New York neighborhood.

BEST FOOT FORWARD

In 1963, Walken began a successful run as Clayton "Dutch" Miller in this off-Broadway revival of a popular 1941 **musical**. He quit college to appear in the show, for which he earned $55 a week. While *Best Foot Forward* is best remembered today as Liza Minnelli's New York theatrical debut, the *New York Times* saved its most effusive praise for Walken, calling him "a handsome fellow with plenty of zest and aplomb."

BILOXI BLUES ★★★

In one his most memorable supporting performances, Walken plays the crazed drill sergeant, Merwyn J. Toomey, in this 1988 big-screen adaptation of Neil Simon's Tony Award-winning Broadway play. Matthew Broderick plays Eugene Jerome, Simon's alter ego, a virginal Army recruit who learns the ropes in basic training during World War II. Director Mike Nichols brought in a real-life drill sergeant to work with Walken on body language and military vernacular. The training sessions paid off in a performance that is as natural as it is fun to watch. Walken really looks at home browbeating his recruits—and his periodic wig-outs are effectively underplayed to suit the material. The film's climactic scene called for Walken to menace Matthew

AS AN ECCENTRIC DRILL SERGEANT, WALKEN BEDEVILS AN IMPRESSIONABLE MATTHEW BRODERICK IN NEIL SIMON'S *BILOXI BLUES*.

Broderick with a handgun, which provided the perfect opportunity for Walken to pull the "Get me the other **gun**" prank that Sean Penn had used on him two years earlier while filming *At Close Range.*

Neil Simon, who was on the set throughout, came away favorably impressed with Walken's performance. During one scene, in which Toomey berates one of his vulnerable soldiers at length, Walken improvised at rehearsal, never once delivering a line as Simon had written it. Afterwards, he apologized to the playwright, saying "I'm sorry. I got carried away." "No, no," Simon replied. "It was magnificent. Infinitely better than what I wrote. Please use it in the scene instead." Walken shook his head. "No. Sometimes I have to do that to clarify in my own mind what exactly the speech is about. Now I know. Your words are better, believe me. I really want to say it as written. Besides," he added, "I'd never remember what I ad-libbed in a million years."

> *"I have a nutcracker that crunches the testicles of men that take me on."*
>
> — Sgt. Merwyn J. Toomey to one of his rebellious charges in 1988's *Biloxi Blues*

BISEXUALITY

Walken played a bisexual Bassanio in a gay-themed interpretation of **Shakespeare**'s *The Merchant of Venice* at the Repertory Theater of Lincoln Center in 1973. In an interview promoting the play, he admitted that he drew upon his own sense of sexual identity in crafting the character. "I suppose I think of the man I'm playing as bisexual, and I suppose that's how I think of myself, too," Walken told *After Dark* magazine. "I'd hate to think that I was harnessed to heterosexuality. I mean, my life is heterosexual, but I like to think that my head is bisexual, and I think it's a good idea for everybody to start getting used to that notion, because that way one becomes aware of a lot more things."

Andy Warhol raised the issue of Walken's purported bisexuality in a March 1985 diary entry in which he reports having seen Walken kiss fellow thespian Mickey Rourke on the lips at a party for producer Dino De Laurentis. "Actors do kiss each other," Walken later told *Playboy* magazine. "I don't think there's anything going on between me and Mickey. Sounds like a nice book."

BLACK

This hue is Walken's sartorial color of choice. "I wear a lot of black because I think it's attractive, but also because it looks neat and clean and sensible. Hundreds of millions of Asians wear black. They know what they're doing."

BLADE RUNNER

Walken was briefly considered for the role of Rick Deckard, the jaded protagonist of director Ridley Scott's neo-noir adaptation of Phillip K. Dick's novel *Do Androids Dream of Electric Sheep?* At this early stage of pre-production, Tommy Lee Jones and Dustin Hoffman were also in the running for the part, which eventually went to Harrison Ford. With **Han Solo**, that makes two enduring sci-fi icons Ford "stole" from Christopher Walken.

BLAST FROM THE PAST   ★★★

In interviews, Walken has often expressed his desire to play more "wise father" roles in the manner of *My Three Sons* patriarch Fred MacMurray. In 1999's *Blast from the Past*, he gets his chance. Not surprisingly, he gives this doting 1960s dad a decidedly daffy Walkenesque spin. Hugh Wilson directs this amiable fish-out-of-decade comedy, about a married couple (Walken and Sissy Spacek) who seek refuge in a bomb shelter during the Cuban Missile Crisis. Convinced that the world has been rendered uninhabitable by a nuclear holocaust, they raise their son (Brendan Fraser) on a combination of mom-and-apple-pie bromides and reruns of *The Honeymooners*. When he ventures up to the surface to seek provisions after thirty-five years underground, comic and romantic complications ensue.

As Kennedy–era householder Calvin Webber—a man who boils his Dr. Pepper among a host of other eccentricities—Walken is out-fitted in a severe brush cut and horn-rimmed glasses and given free

WALKEN CUTS A RUG WITH HIS OLD PAL SISSY SPACEK
IN THE 1999 COMEDY *BLAST FROM THE PAST*.

rein to indulge his flair for unconventional line reading. He also has terrific chemistry with Spacek, an old friend from their early acting days in New York. Together, she and Walken dominate the first third of the movie, playing an almost-but-not-quite-frightening Cold War couple that director Hugh Wilson likened to "Ozzie and Harriet on acid." (See **LSD**.)

Walken was pleased with his work on *Blast from the Past*, which pre-figures his transition to fatherly roles that would culminate in 2002's *Catch Me If You Can*. "For the kinds of parts that I usually play, it was a very nice departure," he declared at the time of *Blast's* release. Also giving thumbs up to Walken's work as Calvin Webber was costar Brendan Fraser. A huge fan of *The Dead Zone*, the lantern-jawed actor called Walken "an entertainer of the highest order" and came away impressed by his costar's idiosyncratic approach to acting—not to mention his diet. "He seemed very cryptic, but beneath it, he had a wry sense of humor," Fraser admitted to an interviewer. "At the reading when I met him, he was eating a bowl of jalapeño peppers as if they were lozenges! And I thought, 'That's my dad!'" Fraser also provided eyewitness testimony to one of Walken's favorite on-set rituals: lemon sucking. "He'd suck lemons before he had to speak a mouthful of dialogue. So there were little chewed-up lemon wedges hidden all over the set, in his pockets, in his bathroom. And he ate a lot of garlic, too."

"What happened to my backyard?"

—Calvin Webber, expressing his exasperation at the sorry state of "post-nuclear" America
in 1999's *Blast from the Past*

BLONDIE AND PENNY

Names of the two mixed-breed dogs owned by Walken and his brothers when he was a child.

BODY ODOR

According to Dan Fogler, Walken's costar in *Balls of Fury*, Walken has a very distinctive personal aroma. "He's got a certain smell, a real Walken-y kind of smell," Fogler told MTV. Pressed on the exact nature of that smell, Fogler likened it to "lilac and orange peels." Others have picked up a slightly different bouquet. Writing about Walken for *Details* magazine, Erik Hedegaard observed that "At all times he reeks of garlic."

BRAINSTORM ★★

Fresh off his moneymaking star turn in *The Dogs of War*, Walken took on another leading man role in this big-budget sci-fi melodrama from special effects wizard turned director Douglas Trumbull. Screen legend **Natalie Wood** costarred in the 1983 feature, in what would be her final big-screen appearance. Wearing a skinny tie and big glasses typical of the early 80s, Walken plays Dr. Michael Anthony Brace, a brilliant scientist whose latest breakthrough is "The Hat," a virtual reality helmet that allows its wearer to experience the sensations and emotions of other people. Wood is his estranged wife, whose feelings for him are rekindled by the aforementioned headgear. The film is turgid at times, with bad acting all around, and visual effects that are as dated as the Atari 2600. But as slices of Reagan Era sci-fi cheese go, it's better than *Tron* and just a notch below *War Games*. Critics were uniformly uncharitable. Writing in *Time* magazine, Richard Schickel faulted Walken for the "charmless introspection" of his character," which, he claimed, "seems perversely calculated to put the audience off."

Although his reputation for intensity preceded him, Walken tried to keep things light during filming. "He made me laugh a lot," reported co-star Louise Fletcher, who played Brace's tightly wound research partner. "Right before the scene would start, he

AFTER DONNING "THE HAT," WALKEN TAKES A VIRTUAL
REALITY MIND TRIP IN *BRAINSTORM*.

would do something completely different just to get the energy
going, like he'd drop his pants or something." That may not have
been the only time he dropped trou on the *Brainstorm* set. Rumors
abounded that Walken and Wood were having an affair away from
the cameras. The fires of innuendo were further stoked when
Walken turned up on the boat with Wood and her husband,
Robert "R. J." Wagner, on the weekend she drowned in November
1981. After a night of drunken revelry, Walken and Wagner reportedly had a loud argument shortly before Wood disappeared from

the boat, never to return. She was found floating in the waters off Catalina Island several hours later. An official investigation concluded her death was an accident, probably caused by intoxication. Walken has largely maintained radio silence about the incident over the years, "out of respect for the family."

BRAZZI, ROSSANO

Brazzi is the Italian actor on whom Walken modeled his portrayal of Robert, the Venetian sadist, in *The Comfort of Strangers.* "I listened to a number of Rossano Brazzi movies—put his voice on my tape recorder and walked around with that for a while. I always liked Rossano Brazzi very much, and the way he spoke—he had a terrific way of speaking English. I don't know how close I got, but his voice was the one I referred to."

BROADWAY DANNY ROSE

This 1984 Woody Allen comedy, about a bumbling talent agent who runs afoul of some gangsters, is one of Walken's favorite movies. He may be attracted by the film's unglamorous portrayal of a low-rent New York show business milieu, a scene that Walken knows well from his early days as a child actor.

BUGS BUNNY

Walken is a big fan of the wisecracking cartoon hare with the distinctive New York accent. "He's so smart, he's so funny, he's got such a great attitude. Bugs Bunny is the spirit of New York," Walken has said. "You can't fool Bugs Bunny. That's all I have to say. He's on to everybody." Walken has admitted that he sometimes reads out his part in a script in a Bugs Bunny voice to get into character.

"I think Bugs Bunny is one of the most interesting movie characters of all time. His rhythms, his intelligence, his attitude is very amazing."

—Walken, on his love for Bugs Bunny

BUNGEE JUMPING

A cautious man by nature, Walken has no patience for people who engage in high-risk activities like bungee jumping. "There are things that are dangerous; you shouldn't do them. I mean, I look at someone bungee jumping, and I think: 'There goes another asshole.' Or parachute jumping, for that matter. Unless you're dropping behind enemy lines, I really don't see the need for it."

BUSINESS AFFAIR, A   ★★

Of all the characters he's played, Walken has called Vanni Corso, the brash publishing magnate he portrays in this 1994 feature, the one most like himself in real life. If that's true, you have to feel bad for the actor's friends and family, because Corso is a boorish, amoral scoundrel with few if any redeeming qualities. Set in London, **England**, *A Business Affair* depicts a love triangle involving Corso—an American arriviste trying to make his name in the world of highbrow literary fiction—his star author (Jonathan Pryce) and the author's aspiring writer wife (Carole Bouquet). A sexually rapacious bounder, Walken steals Bouquet's affections with his skills in the bedroom (the "Nijinsky of cunnilingus," she calls him), thereby making a mortal enemy of Pryce (who dubs him "a human sebaceous cyst with dyed hair"). Complications, both professional and personal, ensue.

Amping up his New York accent by a few hundred notches, Walken delivers an agreeably buffoonish performance—although it's not quite enough to keep this mildly diverting romantic soufflé from falling somewhat flat. Still, it's worth a look to see him golfing in argyles and tangoing with abandon in a nightclub scene. "I thought it was a good part, a big part, a nice sympathetic character in a way," he observed at the time, "and also it was something to do with a woman, which I don't usually get." Critics weren't quite so impressed. The *New York Times* called *A Business Affair* "a pleasant trifle." *Variety*, while praising the film's "tasteful" use of nudity (Bouquet's, not Walken's, praise God), noted that the "deliberately deglamorizing lighting is unflattering to all concerned," and the "accordion-heavy score . . . rarely suits the action."

BUTT DOUBLE

In October of 2007, the celebrity news blog Starpulse.com reported that Walken demanded a "butt double" during filming of the 2008 feature *Five Dollars a Day*. According to the report, the actor was mortified to discover a scene in the script that called for him to "drop trou" on camera. Producers scrambled to audition doubles whose derrieres could plausibly pass for Walken's own. "Men lined up to get Polaroids taken," confided an on-set source.

JS SKETCH . CELLULOIDE . "COLESLAW FOR EVERYBODY
DEL COWARD . CATS . THE DOGS OF WAR . SUSA
INKERBELLE" CAMPBELL . COMMUNION . CLEANLINES
TCH ME IF YOU CAN . JOHN "CHA CHA" CIARCIA . DAY
ONEMENT . DUCK JOKE . "COLESLAW FOR EVERYBODY!" .
UNTRY BEARS . COOKING . DRUGS . RENZO CESANA . BRAN
E WILDE . THE DEAD ZONE . CALIGULA . CATCH ME IF YOU
ATS . JOHN "CHA CHA" CIARCIA . CHARLIE ROSE . DRIVI
OWBELL SKETCH . CHILDHOOD . CATCH ME IF YOU CAN . CLE
NESS . DANNY DANIELS . THE DEER HUNTER . DUCK JO
EADLINE . SUSANNA "TINKERBELLE" CAMPBELL . THE DOGS
AR . THE CONTINENTAL . CHARLIE ROSE . CHILDHOOD . DON
AMMELL'S . WILD SIDE . MONTGOMERY CLIFT . DOMIN
COLESLAW FOR EVERYBODY!" . DANNY DANIELS . COOKING .
OMFORT OF STRANGERS . DRUGS . OLGA . COMEDY HO
MES DEAN . CLIFF . COWBELL AND CENSUS SKETCH . DEADLI
ONALD COLMAN . COMMUNION . THE CONTINENTAL . CALIG
THE DEER HUNTER . COOKING . THE COUNTRY BEARS . CA
DEL COWARD . THE DEAD ZONE . DANCE . DANNY DANIE
OOKING COWBELL SKETCH . RENZO CESANA . COOKING V
HRIS . CORIOLANUS . MONTGOMERY CLIFT . CATS .
UNTRY BEARS . CENSUS SKETCH . DAY OF ATONEMENT . D
KE . CALIGULA . DOMINO . BRANDON DE WILDE . MONTGOM
IFT . DEADLINE . JAMES DEAN . CELLULOIDE . CHRISTOPH
OOKING . THE COMFORT OF STRANGERS . DRUGS .
UNTRY BEARS . SUSANNA "TINKERBELLE" CAMPBELL . CI
ATS . THE DEAD ZONE . THE CONTINENTAL . COMMUNI

C TO D

CALIGULA

In an early indication of his talent for playing villainous characters, Walken took on the role of ancient Rome's blood-soaked boy emperor in this 1971 production of Albert Camus's play at the Yale Repertory Theater in New Haven, Connecticut. Reviewers were divided on the merits of the spare, minimalist staging, and by Walken's performance. The *New York Times*'s reviewer Mel Gussow conceded that "Walken is an articulate actor, and there are moments when he seems on the verge of comprehending *Caligula*" but faulted him for overemphasizing the physical aspects of the role. Especially alarming was a scene late in the play when Walken as Caligula literally crawled across the stage on all fours. "By the end of the drama he is playing bent-over-backwards— skittering across the stage crabwise," Gussow observed. Writing in the same paper a few days later, Gussow's colleague Walter Kerr disagreed. He called Walken's performance "cohesive and chilling" and raved that "he makes philosophy walk." Or crawl, as the case may be.

CAMPBELL, SUSANNA "TINKERBELLE"

This celebrity scenester of the 1970s claimed to have had a sexual encounter with Walken.

See also **Warhol, Andy**.

CATCH ME IF YOU CAN ★★★

"I'd like to play somebody's father and not have to shoot them," Walken once told an interviewer. With *Catch Me If You Can*, he got his wish, snagging his second Oscar nomination for his crackerjack supporting performance in this 2002 feature, directed by Steven Spielberg.

As Frank Abagnale Sr., the downwardly mobile father of an infamous real-life con man played by Leonardo DiCaprio, Walken gives one of his most subtle and assured performances. Walter Parkes, the president of Amblin Entertainment, Spielberg's production company, originally suggested Walken for the part. "I have been a great admirer of Christopher Walken and have always had a desire to work with him," the director later recalled, "so the minute Walter said, 'Have you ever considered Chris Walken?' everything came into focus about who should play Leonardo DiCaprio's father." Despite having such high-powered support in his corner, Walken almost didn't get the part because of his reluctance to attend a face-to-face meeting with Spielberg and DiCaprio. Costar Tom Hanks had to intervene to set up the impromptu audition.

Once he had the part secured, Walken turned to an unlikely source for inspiration. "I'm a big **Jerry Lewis** fan. I heard him say once in an interview that his big secret is he's only nine. That all his life he's only been nine years old, and I thought, yes, absolutely. He's like a kid. You get that feeling with certain people. Mick Jagger has that. I think that's a wonderful quality, especially as you get older. I did get the feeling that Frank Abagnale Sr. and his son were like a couple of juvenile delinquents." Keying on Frank's mischievous nature would turn out to be all the research Walken needed to complete the portrayal. He admits to never having read the book on which *Catch Me If You Can* was based or seeking out any information on the man he was playing. One day the real Frank Abagnale Jr. even dropped by the set; Walken inquired about his father's health and was surprised to learn that Frank Abagnale Sr. had been dead for almost thirty years. "It never even occurred to me," Walken confessed.

There are a lot of great Walken moments in *Catch Me If You Can*, but two in particular bear his personal stamp. An early scene in the script called for Abagnale Sr. to **dance** with his wife on Christmas Eve. Walken choreographed his own dance moves—including a dip. "People don't do dips anymore," he pointed out. Later in the film, Abagnale and son meet up for a drink and Walken's character chokes up while reminiscing about his ex-wife. Leonardo DiCaprio has

WALKEN EARNED HIS SECOND OSCAR NOMINATION FOR HIS PORTRAYAL OF
FRANK ABAGNALE SR. IN STEVEN SPIELBERG'S *CATCH ME IF YOU CAN*.

called this final scene together "one of my most memorable experiences making films." Walken's improvisation caught the younger
actor by surprise. "I thought the man was having a heart attack in
front of me. I honestly was about two seconds away from saying, 'Cut!
There's something wrong with Chris!' It's a testament to how he is
as an actor. I was blown away."

Also blown away were BAFTA, the Screen Actors Guild Award
and the National Society of Film critics, all of whom honored
Walken as Best Supporting Actor for his work in this film.

"I don't usually play dads. I play guys who want to dominate the world with uranium."

—Walken, summing up his Oscar-nominated performance in *Catch Me If You Can* for
late night host Jay Leno.

CATS

The consummate cat person, Walken has kept felines as pets for most
of his adult life. "They're so interesting, and not only that, they're low
maintenance," he once observed. He and his wife Georgianne keep
multiple Abyssinians at their home in Connecticut, which they allow
to run wild because Walken abhors the idea of spaying and declaw-
ing. The actor occasionally turns to his pets for a form of pain relief.
"As I get older, my hands hurt," he says. "And I find that when I rub
the cats, it feels better." He also identifies with the animals' less than
social nature. "I've noticed the only thing cats are really interested in
are other cats. And sometimes I think that's true with actors."

Walken is such a feline fan he once wrote the introduction to a
book about cat care (see *KISS Guide to Cat Care*). His passion for
kitties has also impacted his film career in unexpected ways. Actress
Nathalie Baye, who played Walken's wife in *Catch Me If You Can*,
credits Walken's penchant for talking to cats on the set with helping her
overcome her fear of working with him. On another occasion, director Peter Berg recalls visiting Walken's home to try to convince him to
join the cast of Berg's film *The Rundown*. A large cat immediately
sprung onto Berg's lap and "I didn't want to make it seem like I didn't
like his pet because I really wanted him to do my movie." After an hour
or so of negotiation, Walken agreed to play the part. He also confessed
he had no idea whose cat it was. "The thing was a little stinky," Berg
says. "It had long claws. All I could do at that point is look at Chris and
say, 'This is not your cat?'" Walken admitted that the animal must

have wandered in off the street. "I thought your interaction with the animal was so interesting that I didn't want to interrupt it."

IF I ONLY HAD A TAIL

Walken owns **cats**. He's played a cat (see ***Puss in Boots***). And many critics have remarked on his cat-like qualities. So it should come as no surprise that he pines for a certain feline appendage. In an interview with the *New Zealand Herald* in 2005, Walken expressed his belief that acting would be much easier if only actors had tails: "A tail is so expressive. On a cat you can tell if they're annoyed. You can tell whether they're scared. They bush their tail. If I was an actor and I had to play scared in a movie all I'd have to do is bush my tail. I think that if actors had tails it would change everything."

CELLULOIDE　　　★★

This little-seen 1996 Italian feature from director Carlo Lizzani is one of the more obscure films in the Walken canon. Shot on location in Rome, it chronicles the making of Roberto Rossellini's *Open City*, the film credited with ushering in the era of Italian neo-realistic cinema after World War II. Walken hams it up in a cameo role as Rod Geiger, an American army officer who disrupts the production after he learns that Rossellini is stealing electricity from a nearby USO center.

CENSUS SKETCH

Walken plays an affectless apartment dweller with an amorous bobcat for a wife in this agreeably surreal *Saturday Night Live* sketch, which originally aired on April 8, 2000. Tim Meadows plays the census taker who knocks on Walken's door one day with a few simple questions. Walken's increasingly eccentric replies include revelations about nail salon permits, novelty passports, and a recent prison stay. As usual, the sketch wouldn't be half as funny with another actor playing Walken's role. As it is, it's probably the best *SNL* sketch he's ever appeared in—with apologies to **cowbell** enthusiasts.

CESANA, RENZO

This Italian-born actor is better known by the name of his most famous character—**the Continental**. Cesana played the suave, apartment-dwelling lothario in a series of 15-minute television segments from 1952 to 1953. He provided the basis for Walken's less romantically adept take on the character in a recurring *Saturday Night Live* sketch beginning in 1990. Cesana's character also supplied the inspiration for Walken's portrayal of foppish gay theater critic Umberto Bevalaqua in the 1998 feature *Illuminata*.

CHARLIE ROSE

The nightly PBS gabfest, hosted by the eponymous Tar Heel telejournalist, is Walken's favorite **television** show.

CHILDHOOD

Walken has called his **1950s** show business upbringing "an unusual childhood, but a great one. A total education of another sort." With his brothers **Ken** and **Glenn**, he formed a veritable tag team of child actors, appearing on such shows as *Howdy Doody*, *Philco TV Playhouse*, and the *Colgate Comedy Hour*. When one of the brothers couldn't show up for a role, another would fill in for him. "Occasionally I'd have a line that I'd forget," Walken recalls. "My brothers were better at it than I was . . . much." Being interchangeable gave the Walken boys an edge on the other child performers, especially in an era when kids were considered little more than set dressing. "In those days all TV was 'See the USA in your Chevrolet,'" Walken has said. "It was so family-oriented and wholesome that they used kids like furniture. They'd have a scene and—particularly in the holidays—they'd just stick a bunch of kids in there. They just had us there because everybody loves kids."

CHRISTOPHER

Name suggested to Walken in the mid-1960s by nightclub singer **Monique Van Vooren**, after he informed her he didn't like the sound of his real name, Ronald. "I was very young and maybe I thought the new name sounded more romantic," Walken told the *Los Angeles Times* in 1981. In another interview, while acknowledging that his **childhood** friends and family still call him **Ronnie**, Walken expressed a desire to shorten his stage name even further. "Anybody who met me after I was 25 calls me Chris," he observed. "I asked my agent if I could change my billing to Chris Walken. It's what everybody calls me, and it takes up less space. It's easier to say. But people don't like change. Producers say, 'If I paid for the full name, I'm getting the full name.'" On another occasion, Walken mused about the possibility of scrapping **Christopher** altogether. "I don't really care for it," he said. "It doesn't suit me. I need something more to the point, a little dark. Jack. Nick."

> *"Christopher sounds like a sneeze.*
> *Short names are more sexy."*
>
> —Walken, on why he prefers to be called Chris

CIARCIA, JOHN "CHA CHA"

This Little Italy restaurateur is an occasional Walken collaborator. *See also Cooking with Chris.*

CLEANLINESS

An avowed neat freak, Walken calls cleanliness "an absolute necessity."
"Everybody should be that way. . . . I'm very clean. I don't like things
that aren't cleaned up. But I hardly use soap at all. I don't use a lot of
soap because it makes me feel sticky. I don't like to use it in my hair—
I usually just run it under the water." Although Walken denies that he
suffers from obsessive compulsive disorder, his neatness fixation put
the kibosh on his one and only attempt at talk therapy in the 1970s.

See also **Analysis**.

CLICK   ★★

The angel of death wears a fright wig in this high-concept 2006
comedy starring Adam Sandler, Kate Beckinsale, and a shamelessly
hammy Walken. He plays Morty, a wisecracking celestial puppetmas-
ter who moonlights in the back room at a Bed Bath & Beyond. For
reasons known only to him, he takes an interest in the life of a
self-absorbed shlub (Sandler) who habitually ignores his wife and
children. Walken gives Sandler a magical remote control that allows
him to fast forward and rewind through his own life, with predictably
comic consequences. The film's central conceit is a clever one—
although it was largely lost on the technophobic Walken. "I have a
remote but I'm always pushing some button that turns everything
off, and if my wife is not home when it happens, I have to wait till
she comes home."

Click lifts elements from *A Christmas Carol*, *Slaughterhouse-Five*,
It's a Wonderful Life, and about a half dozen *Twilight Zone* episodes
before wheezing to its overwrought finale. Walken has some fun
with his role—essentially a variation on Christopher Lloyd as Doc
Brown in *Back to the Future*—although it's hard to buy him in the
more serious scenes given his outlandish costume and finger-in-
the-socket hairstyle. Still, if it rings your bell to see Walken and

WALKEN CONSIDERS PUTTING ADAM SANDLER OUT OF
HIS MISERY IN THE INTERMINABLE COMEDY *CLICK*.

Sandler **dancing** together to "Give Up the Funk" by Parliament, this is the film for you.

On the set, Walken's freewheeling spirit seems to have had a positive effect on his costars. "Every day was pretty enjoyable," Adam Sandler remarked, "although my favorite part of it all was introducing people to Christopher Walken. The fear in their eyes. It's like no one knows what will happen." Kate Beckinsale agreed: "I remember my young daughter running into him on the set. The whites of her eyes were huge. She came back to me and said, 'Mommy, I've just seen a man I don't like.' But then, when she got to know him, well, she warmed right up to him."

CLIFT, MONTGOMERY

This moody Method actor of the 1950s and 60s was an obvious precursor to Walken—especially late in Clift's career, when he became known for delivering compelling, idiosyncratic performances in relatively small parts. Walken met Clift shortly before he died in 1966. "I sat next to him for half an hour before I realized who he was," he told an interviewer in 1977. "We had the most terrific conversation that you could have without saying anything. We sat there. There was nobody else around. I had nothing to say to him. He had nothing to say to me. We drank, smoked cigarettes and didn't speak." After a while, Walken simply got up and left.

"COLESLAW FOR EVERYBODY!"

This strange phrase is apparently some kind of personal rallying cry for Walken. Obscure in origin, its first use dates to 1985, when Walken reportedly shouted it from a rooftop to a crowd of gawkers on the set of the **James Bond** movie *A View to a Kill*. The phrase also turns up in Walken's 1996 cyberpunk film *New Rose Hotel*, during a presumably improvised dinner scene between Fox (Walken) and X (Willem Dafoe). As the two men discuss their plan to send a call girl to seduce a brilliant geneticist, Walken suddenly and seemingly nonsensically blurts out "Coleslaw for everybody!"

COLGATE COMEDY HOUR

At a 2004 career retrospective held at the Film Society of Lincoln Center, Walken credited his 1953 appearance on this program with inspiring him to pursue a career in show business. The then ten-year-old Walken appeared in a skit with guest hosts Dean Martin and **Jerry**

Lewis. The scene called for Lewis to wrestle frantically with an arm sticking out of a wall at a penny arcade. Walken played one of a crowd of children laughing at him. In subsequent interviews, he has often cited Lewis as a major influence, particularly in his contention that all actors are essentially nine years old at heart.

COLMAN, RONALD

Walken was named Ronald after this debonair British actor, best known for his Oscar-winning portrayal of a homicidal actor in the 1947 film noir *A Double Life*.

COLONEL ANGUS SKETCH

Recycling a gag it had used twenty-five years earlier, *Saturday Night Live* cast Walken as the smuttily named Confederate officer Colonel Ennol Angus in this February 22, 2003 sketch. An extended—some might say overextended—double entendre on the word *cunnilingus*, Colonel Angus echoes the "Colonel Lingus" fried chicken ad read by Don Pardo on November 4, 1978. In its original iteration, the bit lasted only ten seconds. This one seems to go on forever, with Walken looking somewhat lost in a fake beard and grey Rebel uniform. His attempt to do a Southern accent is amusing, however—more amusing than the rest of the sketch. Expect a skit about "Colonel Inga's House of Sauerbraten" to pop up sometime in 2028.

COMFORT OF STRANGERS, THE   ★★★★

If **The Continental** were a homicidal pervert living in Venice, he'd be a lot like Robert, the character Walken plays in this dark erotic odyssey. Released in 1990, *The Comfort of Strangers* boasted a stellar creative pedigree. Playwright Harold Pinter adapted the script from Ian McEwan's novel, with *Taxi Driver* and *Raging Bull* screenwriter Paul Schrader in the director's chair. Walken and Helen Mirren play

"COLONEL ANGUS" DROPS A FEW RIBALD PUNS ON THE *SATURDAY NIGHT LIVE* CAS

a pair of aristocratic Venetian whack jobs who lure a vacationing young English couple (Rupert Everett and Natasha Richardson) into their web of violence and kink, with deadly consequences. In a mesmerizing performance that suggests his true calling is to one day play Count Dracula, Walken deftly mixes old-world sophistication with vampirish creepiness. He has called Robert "the most mentally unhealthy person I've ever played, which says a lot." To achieve the desired effect, Walken put on twenty pounds for the part, something he admitted he has never done for any other movie.

A steady diet of the local Italian cuisine made that easy. "It's better, when you're an actor, to go some place where the **food**'s not so good," Walken has said. "Next time you see [*The Comfort of Strangers*], check. I'm pretty porky."

After larding up on pasta, Walken sought further inspiration for his portrayal in the realm of fairy tales. He likened the plot of *Comfort of Strangers* to the story of *Hansel and Gretel*, with the innocent couple played by Everett and Richardson lured into the clutches of an evil "witch" in the form of Robert. His other innovation was to keep his hands in his pockets in nearly every scene, to highlight the concealed menace of his character. Once he had locked onto Robert's Mephistophelean essence, however, Walken needed no further assistance from technical trickery. During one pivotal scene, Schrader announced his intention to light Walken's face from below to create a sinister glow. Walken demurred, declaring: "I don't need to be made to look evil. I can do that on my own!"

He was right. Walken is perfectly diabolical throughout, so much so that he scared himself. He caught a glimpse of his face in his dressing room mirror one day and literally recoiled at his own reflection. "I had exactly the same reaction that I would have if I was in a restaurant and saw somebody I absolutely did not want to see. I looked up and quickly looked away, thinking, I hope he leaves, I hope he didn't see me."

> ### "He really disturbed me. I was glad to say goodbye to Robert."
>
> —Walken, reflecting on his performance as a nattily-dressed Venetian pervert in
> *The Comfort of Strangers*

COMMUNION   ★★★

Walken survives an **anal probing** in this 1989 film about alien abduction, based on the (purportedly) real-life experiences of novelist Whitley Strieber. Walken plays Strieber as a loving husband and devoted father—albeit with a few writerly eccentricities, such as wearing a fedora around the house for no particular reason—who suddenly and dramatically goes bonkers after little blue men start showing up at his upstate New York country home. He flips out and nearly blows his wife away with a shotgun, but instead of having him committed she sends him to see a high-toned shrink (Frances Sternhagen) who runs a UFO abductee encounter group. Walken is at his over-the-top best in scenes where he recalls his alien encounters under hypnosis. "How dare you?" he seethes as the aliens snake a long hose up his rectum. In other scenes he's shown boogeying down with the apparently disco-crazed spacemen and making cryptic pronouncements like "I am he and you are he and we are here." The aliens, played by midgets in little rubber suits, look like refugees from the cantina scene in *Star Wars*. It's jolly good fun, although the point of all this probing and dancing remains obscure, and Walken seems a bit miscast as a supposedly boring middle class househusband. Even Strieber himself had a hard time buying Walken in the role. When he informed Walken that he might be playing the character a tad too crazy, Walken replied "If the shoe fits" and went on with the show.

Walken has called Whitley Strieber (who co-produced and adapted the screenplay from his bestselling book) "a fascinating guy." In a departure from his usual process, Walken spent some time with his real-life counterpart to prepare for the role. "He's like a radio show. He does the sounds and the screams. Whitley has people come over to his house, people who had the same thing happen to them, and they all agree about what the aliens looked like. And they all seem perfectly . . . well, they all have jobs." As to whether the abduction depicted in the film actually took place, Walken demurs. "I believed that he believed. And I think it'd be a gas if aliens came and said hi. Wouldn't that be great?"

Despite Walken's best efforts, however, *Communion* bombed at the box office. A proposed sequel, based on Strieber's follow-up book *Transformations*, never got off the ground. Even if it had, it likely wouldn't have starred Walken. "We found with *Communion* that nobody really accepted Christopher Walken as playing Whitley," observed producer Michael Nelson, "because he's just a bit too creepy for words." Plans were in the works to replace Walken with former televangelist Jim Bakker, and later SCTV and *Honey, I Shrunk the Kids* alum Rick Moranis, but they never came to fruition. Further probing will have to wait for another day.

> *"Little blue fuckers—about that big."*
>
> — Whitley Strieber, describing the aliens who probed him, in 1989's *Communion*

CONTINENTAL, THE

"More people probably know me as the Continental on *Saturday Night Live* than they do from any movie I did," Walken has admitted. One shudders to imagine that statement's implications for the state of American cultural literacy, but there's no question this bizarre recurring character has struck a chord with late-night comedy viewers. To date, Walken has played the Continental six times. The sketch parodies a **1950s** television series starring Italian actor **Renzo Cesana**. Playing an unnamed playboy who speaks directly to the camera as if it were a woman entering his swank New York apartment, Cesana became known as "the first electronic gigolo" and "the Atomic Age Casanova." Walken's twist is to make the Continental not so much a suave playboy as a lecherous buffoon. His repeated attempts to sweep his lady guest off her feet—or merely spy on her in the bathroom—invariably end in disaster, and usually with a drink thrown in his face. Adding to the comic effect is Walken's strange accent, which blends his native New Yawkese with Eurotrash-tinged invitations to indulge in some "fine shom-pon-ya." The unlikely popularity of the Continental led to speculation that a movie might be made about the character. Walken has long pined for one, but even he understands the character has his limitations. "The problem with the Continental is that he never leaves his house. But it might be interesting to see the Continental go out and nothing works. He's a social catastrophe. I think that would be interesting."

COOKING

Cooking is one of Walken's passions. In fact, he rarely eats out in restaurants because he doesn't want anyone else touching his **food**. "That's just the way I am. I like to know exactly what I'm eating. I like to know what's in it." Cost may also factor into it. "Occasionally I go to these very fancy restaurants on an anniversary or a birthday or something. I don't want to name any names, but I haven't really been knocked out in the last few years. . . . I went to one of the big ones recently. The check was unbelievable. For three people it was like three hundred bucks apiece!"

Instead, Walken prefers to spend that money on quality ingredients and do the preparation in his kitchen while studying scripts. "I put the script on the counter and I cook and study my lines at the same time. It's the power of distraction, I find. I've read that a lot of people do one thing while there's something that they're doing at the same time. Some people play cards or garden. I cook. My wife doesn't cook. That's actually common. I think more men cook than women cook."

So what can you expect should you be invited to dine chez Walken? Walken has described himself as "sort of a Japanese-Italian cook." One of his signature dishes is steamed Chilean sea bass. "I cut the tops of leeks and steam them soft, then lay the sea bass on them and add a little dill, salt, pepper. When you take it out the sea bass flakes off in slabs. Absolutely divine." Roast duck is another one of his specialties. "I make a tremendous duck. You have to steam a duck first. I don't think many people do that. This amazing amount of fat comes off. Then you put it on a rack. You stuff it with garlic and oranges, you know, salt, pepper, some herb, whatever that might be. And you put it on the rack and roast it, and it comes out really crispy. I got that from the Julia Child cookbook. Her cookbooks are wonderful, Julia Child."

When he's away on location, Walken brings his own ingredients along in one of the numerous **Tupperware** containers from his vast collection. He invariably requests that his apartment or hotel room be equipped with a full kitchen so he can prepare his own meals, using lessons he learned early in his show business career. "When I was a kid, I was in **musicals**, and there'd be the dancers, you know, these crazy Gypsies. They'd show up in the little hotel with a suitcase, open it up, and it had every kind of cooking utensil. They would cook these incredible dinners from nothing. Thanksgiving would come and they'd cook this huge turkey in the room. I don't know how they did it."

Even when he's short on cookware, Walken often finds he can make do by planning ahead. He brings a collapsible steamer with him wherever he goes and relies on his mental database of know-how to get him through any situation. "I've had to stay in places where there only was a microwave. It's not recommended, but you can actually cook certain fish in a microwave. Salmon you can cook practically anywhere. And if you're living like a hobo in a hotel room, you can make amazing things in crockpots. You can stick a chicken in there with some vegetables. Turn it on real low and just leave it there all day. And when you come back it's fabulous."

As for advice for those who wish to follow in his footsteps, Chef Chris has two ironclad tenets of culinary wisdom: buy good ingredients and don't overcook. "The real secret is perfect timing—not to cook too long and not too little," he says. "You buy the best stuff you can get and cook it simply, you don't use butter, you use oil, garlic. People spend so much money on pre-cooked, packaged stuff. They don't realize that it's so much cheaper, as well as better, to buy your food and cook it."

> *"There's nothing weird about it. It's common sense. I'm amazed people let total strangers mess around with their food. You'd have to be crazy."*
>
> —Walken, on his reluctance to eat in restaurants

COOKING WITH CHRIS

A dedicated home cook, Walken has long fantasized about hosting his own TV **cooking** show. "It would just be me cooking," he told the *New York Observer.* "Once in a while I'd have a mystery guest. Maybe Joe Pesci comes over and, you know, makes his tomato sauce." Walken also suggested comedian Jay Mohr might make a good sidekick "because I believe everybody's got a dish they can cook. And I want to have an assistant, a huge, statuesque showgirl with very long fingernails. Every time she cuts my vegetables—'cause I need a lot of diced vegetables—she's always slicing off her fingernails. It would be a nightmare. A delicious nightmare."

Sounds great, right? But wait, there's more. In interviews through the years, Walken developed his concept even further, postulating a live audience and musicians and likening the **television** show to *Pee-Wee's Playhouse,* the cult hit children's show starring Paul "Pee

Wee Herman" Reubens. "Or I could do restaurant reviews. Like Ruth Reichl, I could walk in with a big disguise. Like a great big wig. Like everybody would know, they'd be like, 'Oh, here comes Chris with a big wig. Who's he kidding with those big dark glasses?' Or I could dress up like a woman. Get dressed up with a big fur coat, and I could pretend it's not me." He has also repeatedly named Dean Martin's old variety show as a source of inspiration. "I remember Dean Martin's old shows, when he had the Gold Diggers. It was a fabulous show. They say they had the whole thing set up and he'd get in his car and drive from his house, park the car, walk into the studio and do it completely off the cuff. You watch it and you could tell that he didn't really know what was going on. And every time things got a little rough, these showgirls called the Gold Diggers—these gorgeous girls—would come on and do this dance number. That's sort of what I had in mind."

In the late 1990s, Walken actually pursued this idea, setting up meetings with a number of cable networks—including MTV and Bravo—about the proposed series. Sadly, no one bit on his proposal for a raucous, anarchic hour of **cooking** and showgirls. "With the cable, the thing was, when it got down to it, every one of them wanted something much more precise. They wanted it to be much more planned. Much more of a pragmatic, fabricated thing that could be repeated. They wanted to have a comic actor with me. They wanted to have a script. Jokes. I like jokes. But I wouldn't want to have to say the jokes, you know. Because certain times things are funny anyway. I mean, funny people are funny. And I said to them I wouldn't be able to do that. I wanted it to be like the Dean Martin show."

Finally, in 1999, Walken's dream became a reality—sort of—when *Cooking with Chris* aired as a segment on the Independent Film Channel's magazine show *Split Screen*. There were no showgirls, no elaborate wigs, and none of the party atmosphere Walken had in mind, but he did get to cook alongside two of his longtime friends: painter **Julian Schnabel** and Little Italy restaurateur **John "Cha Cha"** Ciarcia, the owner of Cha Cha's In Bocca Al Lupo restaurant on Mulberry Street in New York's Little Italy. The show follows the three men as they go grocery shopping, then decamp to the kitchen at lower Manhattan's Il Cortile restaurant to prepare a light meal. Schnabel, who worked as a cook early in his career, wears a billowy sarong throughout and makes an unusual sandwich out of cream cheese, horseradish, watercress, cucumbers, and bresaola on black bread. In the show's explosive climax, a sautée pan filled with alcohol-doused shrimp catches on fire while astonished kitchen staff look on. Nine hours of video were pared down to the half hour that saw air. "I thought it was entertaining" was Walken's characteristically terse assessment.

Sadly, not enough people shared that conclusion to justify commissioning any additional episodes of *Cooking with Chris*. (For his part, Cha Cha refused to give up on the idea of working with Walken again. "We're gonna ride roller coasters next," he told an interviewer soon after the cooking show went down in flames. "They're gonna film me and Chris riding roller coasters. The two of us. Julian is welcome to come along—but you can only fit two in a roller-coaster car.") By the middle of the next decade, even Walken had given up on the TV cooking show project. "The danger for me is it could be popular," he told the *New York Times* in 2004. "I've tried to have some prestige as an actor, then I'd be the guy with the cooking show."

Instead, Walken has focused on retooling the idea for the Internet. (A short video of him preparing roast chicken with pears circulated the web in 2007.) In a wide-ranging interview with the *New York Observer*, Walken outlined his vision for a Walkenized web **cooking** show:

> If I wasn't so lazy, I'll tell you what I would do. I saw this
> thing on television. This whole thing with people putting

cameras in their house, for the Net. I understand that people outfit their houses with these things, and some guy's girlfriend finds out that she's been naked all over the Internet. You hear about that. If everybody can do it, it can't be that hard. You just need to figure out where to tune in, right? I would need some help with this. I don't quite understand how the Internet works. I don't have a computer. You know, twelve-year-old kids know all about that. I thought I'd get a couple of those cameras and put them in my kitchen in Connecticut and just, you know, turn it on whenever I felt like it. Maybe I would have a particular time of day I would do it, or something like that. You could charge people to take hits, or something like that. And it would just be me cooking. And I thought to make it amusing, I thought I would have a hotline—you know, a red telephone. And they could call and I could give them advice about their love life. I mean silly stuff, personal questions, about them, you know, 'What should I do?' In the old days, there used to be these things—I can't remember what they're called, but it's a Spanish word. Like a bodega, but something else. They'd be on the corners. You could buy a love potion. You could buy, you know, something, if you were mad at somebody, you could buy a hex. They even had aerosol, I remember—you could spray somebody to get them to fall in love with you or something. I could provide services like that. Or just talk while I'm cooking.

"We bought the food, we cooked it, and we ate it."

—Walken, on the tripartite simplicity of his cooking show *Cooking with Chris*

CORIOLANUS

Walken played the title role in this Shakespeare tragedy at New York's Public Theater in 1988 and 1989. "Outfitted in the hip, double-breasted jackets worn by aging pop royalty," according to the *New York Times*, Walken "fulfill[ed] the protagonist's tragic stature." Reportedly, he also fulfilled his own jones for weed. According to the website gossiplist.com, whenever his character wasn't on stage, Walken was smoking pot in the alley behind the playhouse.

COUNTRY BEARS, THE ★★★

Walken received an undeserved Razzie nomination for his supporting performance in this 2002 children's feature, based on a popular Disneyland attraction. His over-the-top portrayal of Reed Thimple III, a villainous banker who tries to foreclose on the home of a group of singing, dancing, banjo-picking bears, is actually quite effective. As Thimple, Walken gets to drive a fancy car with a wrecking ball for a hood ornament, cavort around his office in his underwear to the tune of Bob Dylan's "Everything is Broken," and issue numerous armpit farts designed to amaze the movie's prepubescent target audience. What's not to love? With cameos from Don Henley, Willie Nelson, and Queen Latifah—among many others—*The Country Bears* is a rollicking musical romp and easily Walken's best children's movie since 1988's **Puss in Boots**. Even Walken himself seemed surprised at the negative critical reception: "I liked *The Country Bears*. And I thought I was good in *The Country Bears*. Didn't you think I was funny, with my little shoes?" For real Razzie-worthy Walken acting, see his justly honored work in **Gigli** and **Kangaroo Jack**.

"This isn't ovah! Bears!"

—Reed Thimple III, tasting defeat at the paws of a band of ursine musicians,
in *The Country Bears*

PLAYING A GREEDY BANKER, WALKEN PUTS THE SQUEEZE ON AN URSINE ROCK BAND IN 2002's UNFAIRLY MAGLIGNED *THE COUNTRY BEARS*.

COWARD, NOEL

Walken met the legendary playwright and wit during rehearsals for *High Spirits* in 1964. Walken was appearing in the chorus of the play, a **musical** version of Coward's *Blithe Spirit*. On the first day of rehearsal, Coward made the rounds, stopping to shake the hand of each and every dancer. He did a double take when he got to Walken who was sporting a rather loud fire engine red T-shirt. "Interesting shirt," Coward observed. "Why, yes, it's red," an overwhelmed Walken replied. Coward was unimpressed by this retort. "Well," he sniffed, "it's been an exciting day for us all," and moved along.

COWBELL SKETCH

"I gotta have more cowbell!" With those five words, Walken reinvented his public persona, ushered in a new era in his career, and gave the world an enduring catch phrase. The date was April 8, 2000, during Walken's fourth appearance as host of *Saturday Night Live*. The occasion was a sketch parodying VH1's *Behind the Music*, featuring *SNL* cast members Chris Parnell, Will Ferrell, Horatio Sanz, and Chris Kattan as the members of 1970s rock group Blue Oyster Cult. Walken played "the Bruce Dickinson," a supposedly legendary hitmaker who becomes infatuated with Ferrell's frenetic cowbell playing during the recording sessions for the band's classic "Don't Fear the Reaper." Two elements lift the sketch above the ordinary. One is Ferrell's antic performance (he also wrote the sketch). With his skintight jeans and exposed belly, he's a marvel to watch as the "band" cycles through several lip-synced takes. The other is Walken's weird, affectless delivery of his lines, several of which have entered the pop culture lexicon: "I'm the cock o' the walk, baby," "Really explore the studio space this time," and, of course, "I got a fever. And the only prescription is more cowbell."

Before long, "More Cowbell" was popping up on T-shirts in hipster clothing boutiques and the sketch was being name-checked in numerous songs and movies. A Rochester, NY rock band christened itself More Cowbell in the skit's honor, while a Boston University online community known as the Committee for the Advancement of Cowbell attracted more than one thousand members. There's an entire website devoted to the sketch at www.explorethestudiospace.com. Major League Baseball's Tampa Bay Rays are one of several professional sports teams to display clips from Cowbell on their video board as a way to rally the crowd. Blue Oyster Cult's lead guitarist Donald "Buck Dharma" Roeser has confessed to watching the sketch more than a dozen times. "We're huge Christopher Walken fans," he said on behalf of his fellow band members. (For the record, Ferrell's character, cowbell player Gene Frenkle, is a completely fictional creation.)

"Cowbell" proved to be just the thing Walken needed to help him reinvent himself as a primarily comic actor in the new millennium. After two decades spent playing hitmen, creeps, and weirdos, he was eager to move on to less intense roles. The cowbell sketch, along with the Spike Jonze video for Fatboy Slim's "**Weapon of Choice**," helped introduce Walken to a whole new generation of **fans**. People were soon besieging him with requests to say "More cowbell" into their answering machines—which he did. The sketch's impact was worldwide and lasting. "I was eating in a restaurant in Singapore," Walken observed in 2007, "and an Asian couple was at the next table, and the guy turned to me and he said, 'Chris, you know what this salad needs?' I said, 'What?' He said, 'More cowbell.'"

"Ironically, we don't play any Blue Oyster Cult covers or use much cowbell, either."

—David Laydon, bass player for the Rochester, NY–based band More Cowbell

DANCE

"I think a lot of what Chris does as an actor comes from dance," observed his friend and colleague Meryl Streep. "There are very few actors who train as dancers, and he stands like Baryshnikov—with his chest open like a god.   Juxtaposed with his menace and loose-cannon aspect, it just gives him this crazy beauty."

Walken received his formal dance training as a child, working with legendary tap trainer **Danny Daniels**. He worked primarily as a chorus boy on Broadway well into the 1960s, when he made his dramatic breakthrough in a 1966 production of *The Lion in Winter*. The dancing bug never left him, however. Astute Walken watchers know that the actor often interjects brief dance routines into his movie performances—even when, he admits, it's totally inappropriate to the tone of the film. "It's unprofessional. It's not right. It's unfair to the writer," Walken has confessed. Prime examples of such impromptu jigs can be found in *At Close Range* and *The King of New York*, among many other films. In interviews, Walken has explained this practice as either an homage to his Broadway background or an imitation of street life in his native Queens. "In the summertime, when it was very hot, people would take chairs out and sit on the sidewalk and you'd see these guys do that." Occasionally, he likens his work in dramatic scenes to dance, most famously when discussing his "Sicilian Scene" in *True Romance* with Dennis Hopper: "We danced together. When actors have that flow, and that rhythm, and that give-and-take, they feel each other like a dancer."

DANIELS, DANNY

This legendary Broadway choreographer was Walken's **childhood dance** instructor. He began teaching tap to little Ronnie Walken and his two brothers in the early **1950s** at Jack Stanley's Dance Studio in New York's Roseland Building. The boys spent the better part of two years under Daniels's tutelage.

Even after the lessons ceased, Daniels would continue to play a key role in Walken's burgeoning show business career. In 1963, he recommended Walken and his brother Glenn for parts in the off-Broadway musical *Best Foot Forward*, and he accepted Walken's suggestion that he audition his friend Liza Minnelli for a part in the show as well. The next year, Daniels brought Walken into the chorus for the Broadway musical *High Spirits*, where he described him as "one of my pillars of strength as a dancer. . . . Whenever I needed someone to do an unpleasant task, like manipulating tables and chairs with string, standing in the wings, I asked **Ronnie** to do it and he was always willing, even though at times he was running around backstage like a mad man!"

"FIVE, SIX , SEVEN, EIGHT!" WALKEN TAKES SOME
CUES FROM DANCE TEACHER DANNY DANIELS.

Nearly twenty years later, after Walken had established himself in Hollywood, his association with Danny Daniels paid off one last time, when Daniels recommended him for the role of Tom, the dancing pimp, in Herbert Ross' *Pennies from Heaven*.

DAY OF ATONEMENT   ★

Scarface meets *Sholom Aleichem* in this ponderous 1992 feature about a French-speaking Jewish-American crime family caught up in a misbegotten coke deal with a Chilean-German drug lord. Walken plays Pasco Meisner, a cocaine kingpin, dog-racing enthusiast, and raging anti-Semite who brokers a big-time drug deal with the dysfunctional Bettoun family. The Bettouns are supposed to be major players in the Miami underworld, but they're so riven by simmering family conflicts it's hard to imagine how they stay in business. Walken has a few good scenes, but about halfway through he's reduced to screaming "Where's my coke?" and denouncing all Jews as thieves and liars. In an awkward parody of *The Godfather*, one of Walken's prized racing dogs is killed and thrown into his pool as a warning. That's not the only echo of Francis Ford Coppola's classic. *Day of Atonement*'s interminable opening scene, set at a Bar Mitzvah reception, is a shameless lift of the wedding sequence that opens *The Godfather*. Jill Clayburgh and Jennifer Beals have thankless roles as **women** connected to the Bettoun family. The other actors are all French and uniformly terrible.

> *"You don't give me the coke, I'll hand you your son's head in a plastic garbage bag."*
>
> —Pasco Meisner, outlining the non-negotiable terms of his deal with the Bettoun family, in 1992's *Day of Atonement*

DE WILDE, BRANDON

Walken went to grade school with this child star, best known for his

Oscar-nominated performance opposite Alan Ladd in the classic western *Shane*. According to Walken, De Wilde is the person who taught him how to tie a necktie. He died in a car crash in 1972 at the age of thirty.

DEADLINE ★★

In 1987, Walken left the Broadway production of John Guare's *House of Blue Leaves* to start filming this feature in Tel Aviv. At a time in his career when he was beginning to make the transition from quirky leading man to scene-stealing character actor, *Deadline* (also known as *Witness in the War Zone*) provided a rare showcase for his talents. Walken plays Don Stevens, a jaded telejournalist for the fictional U.S. television network ABS. He covers the Israeli-Palestinian conflict from his hotel in Beirut with all the passion of a fashion correspondent assessing the new fall line—which, incidentally, is what he's just come from doing. The PLO knows a patsy when it sees one, so Stevens soon finds himself enmeshed in a web of intrigue that culminates in a horrific massacre at a Palestinian refugee camp. Hywel Bennett, a dead ringer for Herman's Hermits frontman Peter Noone, plays Stevens' British counterpart, Mike Jessop.

Deadline is a convoluted political thriller that pales in comparison to similarly themed films from the same era, such as *Missing* and *Under Fire*. It has a cheap, grungy look and a pulsating synthesized soundtrack that instantly date it as a mid-1980s production, as does Walken's heinous wardrobe. He strides around war-torn Lebanon in high-waisted slacks and a succession of short-sleeved sport shirts that makes him look like a muckracking Ed Grimley. Even worse for Walken lovers, Don Stevens is one of the most passive, least sympathetic characters the actor has played. His cluelessness and lack of concern for his own safety seemingly know no bounds, as he finds himself shuttled from one perilous situation to another. On the plus side, Walken's **hair** has never looked fuller or more luxuriant. This isn't one of his better films, or better roles, but it does provide a revealing snapshot of the actor at a transitional stage of his career.

"I feel like a one-legged man in an ass-kicking contest."

—Don Stevens, summing up his feelings about his new assignment in Beirut, in 1987's *Deadline*

DEAD ZONE, THE   ★★★★

Stephen King is notoriously hard to please when it comes to adapting his novels for the screen, but even he came away impressed with this 1983 feature, which casts Walken in the lead role of Johnny Smith, a small-town schoolteacher who develops extraordinary psychic powers after a car accident puts him in a coma for five years. Unlike many King films, *The Dead Zone* is quite faithful to the source material, and Walken proves an inspired choice for the protagonist. His subdued otherworldliness fits perfectly here. "In that part I felt really natural," Walken has said. "I behaved and looked and spoke pretty much like myself. The only thing that wasn't like me was his situation. In a case like that I have to just say to myself, what would it be like if this was your life?" Oddly enough, Stephen King originally suggested Bill Murray for the role, while director David Cronenberg favored Canadian actor Nicholas Campbell (who ended up playing Dodd, the serial killing cop). Walken was at Yale appearing in the play *The Philanderer* when Cronenberg summoned him to a meeting to discuss the part. Cronenberg was quickly won over and eventually came to see Walken's creepy visage as the key to the entire picture. "It's Chris Walken's face," Cronenberg later said. "That's the subject of the movie; that's what the movie was about. All the things that are in his face."

VISIONS OF MURDER HAUNT A CLAIRVOYANT WALKEN IN *THE DEAD ZONE*.

Especially effective are the numerous scenes where Smith is jolted into a clairvoyant fugue state at the touch of someone's hand. (At Walken's suggestion, Cronenberg stood just off-camera and fired a .357 Magnum loaded with blanks to make the character's flinches seem more involuntary.) Walken would later spoof this aspect of his performance in a memorable *Saturday Night Live* sketch entitled **"Ed Glosser: Trivial Psychic."** *The Dead Zone* would also find new life in 2002 as a USA Network TV series starring Anthony Michael Hall as Johnny—although Walken himself seemed oblivious to the show's existence. "It's a continuing thing?" he asked an interviewer from *TV Guide* in 2003. "What happens? I keep foreseeing things? What a nightmare!"

> *"The ice . . . is gonna break!"*

—Johnny Smith, imploring a pertinacious tutoring client to cancel his son's ill-starred pond hockey game, in *The Dead Zone*

DEAN, JAMES

The method acting maverick and pop cultural icon is one of Walken's early show business role models. Walken remembers being at a Queens, NY roller-skating rink when he heard the news that Dean had died in a car accident.

DEER HUNTER, THE   ★★★★

If you're going to give the best performance of your career, it pays to do it early. Although his Academy Award-winning portrayal of Pennsylvania steelworker-cum-Vietnam casualty Nick Chevotarevich is rightly considered a starmaker, *The Deer Hunter* was actually Walken's ninth feature film. At the time of its release in December 1978, he was still known primarily as a New York theater actor. Walken was thirty-five years old and seemed resigned to existence as a performer of middling renown. Before *Deer Hunter*, he says, "I was good enough, but I wasn't particularly good. I wasn't ever certain I would be a huge success. I felt okay about that though because I was enjoying life." He'd enjoy it a lot more afterwards. Director Michael Cimino's emotionally wrenching saga earned Walken the Oscar for Best Supporting Actor, remade his financial fortunes, and instantly catapulted him onto the Hollywood A-list for decades to come.

LOOKING READY FOR THE OSCAR BALL, WALKEN PUTS IN
ANOTHER HARD DAY ON *THE DEER HUNTER* SET.

The film follows three working-class steelworkers to Vietnam and back, depicting the emotional and physical scars left behind by their experiences in a Vietcong prison camp. Walken plays Nick, the moony sensualist of the three, whose psychic disintegration drives the film toward its harrowing climax in a Saigon Russian Roulette parlor. The outstanding ensemble cast includes Robert De Niro, John Savage, Meryl Streep, and John Cazale in his final performance. Walken credits Cimino with fostering chemistry on the set, which is evident on screen. "One of the things he did, which was very intelligent, was to cast a lot of theater actors, particularly from New York. There is a sort of camaraderie between actors, and I think it transferred onto film, giving the impression that we'd all been together for a long time."

Walken got the part after meeting personally with Cimino and De Niro. The director—then a relative unknown himself—merely looked Walken over and asked what part he wanted to play. "I named about four of them," Walken recalled later, "but I figured if I was lucky I might get to play Stan, the one that John Cazale played. I never expected him to cast me as Nick. It was just too good a part." His assignation with De Niro was a little more awkward. "We didn't talk much," Walken says of their initial encounter. De Niro did ask whether it was Walken he'd seen recently in a play he liked. It wasn't. Walken considered lying to try to curry favor with his prospective costar, but decided to tell the truth instead. He'd auditioned for the play in question but been turned down. De Niro apparently appreciated his fellow actor's honesty; to this day, Walken believes that exchange got him the part.

Once he secured the gig, Walken began preparing for it by visiting V.A. hospitals to observe real-life Vietnam veterans and how they dealt with the experience of combat. He quickly learned that this kind of research has its limitations. "It didn't do me a bit of good," he concluded, and relied instead on what would become his customary process of finding an approach to the character rooted in his own emotions and experiences. "He was an awful lot like me, in terms of background and personality," Walken has said of Nick. This is especially evident in a critical scene set in a Saigon hospital, where a bewildered Nick sits forlornly by a window, barely able to respond to a doctor's questions. "The day we shot that scene it was very hot, and we had been in Thailand about two weeks . . . I spent the whole time as depressed as I've ever been. I was in the trailer lying around in the heat. I didn't give a thought to the scene. All I was thinking was 'Am I homesick!' I just went and played the scene right then. I was really homesick. I cried and everything, just like I did when I was twelve."

The Thailand shoot was arduous. The heat and humidity in the jungle locations were oppressive, while the accommodations were not exactly four-star. "We stayed in this hotel," Walken recalls, "and at night there'd be a noise. You'd turn on the light and there would be a lizard on the wall, white with big orange dots on it. I'm very squeamish about that stuff. I don't like bugs. But it got to the point where I'd hear a noise, turn on the light, see something on the wall, turn off the light, and go back to sleep." Nevertheless, the unpleasant working conditions fostered a bond among the three male leads. Nowhere is this more apparent than in the exhilarating helicopter rescue sequence, during which Walken and John Savage almost went down to Davy Jones's sampan together. As Walken described the scene to *Film Comment*: "We got in the helicopter, the camera was hand held, and John Savage was behind me and the door was wide open and there was no safety belts or anything. The helicopter took off and went right up, I think a thousand feet—up as high as the Empire State Building. I was look-ing out this door and I said, 'John, grab my belt, hang on to me, do not let go whatever happens.' I couldn't believe I was sitting there, next to this open door without even a rope around me or anything. And the camera was rolling . . . I thought if the helicopter tilted sideways, I'd be gone." Despite sweating like a pig, sleeping with lizards, and nearly losing his life, Walken came away satisfied with his first taste of exotic location filming. "I don't think the movie would have been as compelling if it was done somewhere else," he concluded.

The most compelling scene of all, of course, is the climactic Russian roulette confrontation between De Niro's Mike and Walken's Nick. The sequence is a tour de force for two actors whose on-set intensity and eccentric work habits have become legendary. Filming took place in a cavernous rice storage facility at four in the morning on yet another sweltering day in Southeast Asia. When the two characters meet for the first time after their long separation, Nick spits in Mike's face. At the suggestion of Cimino, Walken's loogie was all too real. "Bob didn't know it was coming," Cimino said later. "And Chris goes, 'You want me to spit in Bob's face? I can't spit in Bob's face!' But he did it. Well, Bob . . . got so angry he almost got out of the scene. But he knew it was working. It's actors like Chris who make scenes like that possible. He's got great courage." De Niro returned the favor a few moments later when Walken came up dry for an idea on how to choreograph the Russian roulette contest. "In the scene where I'm in the gaming room for the first time . . . and I pick up the gun and hold it to my head, he showed me how to do that," Walken has said. "It's a very good moment for me, and I have to admit it's stolen." The final piece of the puzzle also came at De Niro's suggestion. "At one point Bob wanted to put a live round in the gun," Cimino recalled. "And we had a whole conference about 'Okay, we're gonna do it, but we're gonna check this thing five thousand times. We went to a lot of extremes on that film." Live round in the **gun** or no, the moment where Walken puts the pistol to his temple and dies with his head cradled in De Niro's hands is one of the most shocking and powerful in the history of movies. Any hope

Bruce Dern might have had of snatching the Oscar away from Walken was blown away with this "one shot."

The Deer Hunter premiered in Hollywood on December 8, 1978—just in time to be eligible for Academy Award consideration the following March. When it opened wide in February 1979, critical and public response was instant and enthusiastic. "I've never seen men weeping in a movie theater like that," Walken observed. "It sounds like I'm selling the movie, but I'm really surprised; it affects me powerfully too, when I see it. I've never seen people react like that. I've never seen the lights come up after the movie's over and people sit there in sort of stunned silence. Obviously, this is a very unusual and powerful movie." So powerful, in fact, that Walken's own parents called to check on his condition after they saw the film. Not everyone was enamored with the film, of course. Some on the far left and right found fault with its politics. Writing in the *National Review*, John Simon called *Deer Hunter* "the kind of movie dreamed up by kids in a college snack bar over beer and hamburgers." Jane Fonda lambasted what she called its "Pentagon" perspective on the Vietnam War. Walken—along with the majority of moviegoers—disagreed. "I don't think it had anything to do with being about a particular war," he told *Playboy* magazine. "It had more to do with young men's romantic notions of war, the idea that war's an adventure. They think they're going to go and have a good time, get out of the house. In reality, though, they get their legs blown off."

> **"I was lucky. I knew that if I hung around long enough I was bound to get lucky."**
>
> — Walken, on his career-making performance as Nick Chevotarevich
> in *The Deer Hunter*

DOGS OF WAR, THE   ★★★

For his first lead role in a big-budget feature, Walken chose this blood-soaked tale of mercenaries gone wild, based (very loosely) on the bestselling novel by Frederick Forsyth. Released in 1981, the action epic stars Walken as Jamie Shannon, a jaded soldier of fortune who signs on to spearhead a coup against the maniacal leader of the fictional African nation of Zangora. He assembles a team and carries out his mission, but not before springing a few surprises on his unsavory employers. Along the way, Shannon is severely beaten, requiring Walken to perform several scenes in heavy makeup that makes his face look a piece of roughly tenderized beef. "The worst moment was when I came straight back from the set one day with the makeup still on and walked into the hotel lobby. Some tourists had just checked in and they almost fainted at the sight."

You're more likely to nod off than faint if you rent *Dogs of War* today. Sadly, character development was apparently the first casualty of this war, as Walken's creation is little more than a nihilistic killing machine. The climactic assault on the dictator's compound is fun to watch, however, and Walken's kick-ass grenade launcher—an XM18 Manville gun nicknamed "the mean machine"—is the real star of the film, which bears an uncanny resemblance to the superior 1978 movie *The Wild Geese*. One gets the impression everyone involved was too stoned to notice the similarities. Still, if you must see Walken in face paint, blowing away enemies left and right, this is the film for you. "The casting of Walken in the lead gives this picture the fuse it needs," gushed critic Pauline Kael. It also gave Walken the big payday he needed. He told interviewers this was the first film role that earned him any real money.

"Kimba—kick his ass!"

—Jamie Shannon, exhorting his mercenary army to take on a ruthless
African dictator, in 1981's *The Dogs of War*

DOMINO   ★

In his third film for director Tony Scott, Walken plays a manic reality TV show producer in this highly stylized—and extensively fictionalized—account of the exploits of real-life bounty hunter Domino Harvey. Walken's performance is all but lost amidst the headache-inducing video game quick cuts that needlessly assault the viewer throughout this profoundly irritating 2005 film. The target audience appears to be teenagers with attention deficit disorder.

DONALD CAMMELL'S WILD SIDE

See *Wild Side*.

DRIVING

"I've had a license since I was sixteen, and I've never had a ticket," Walken boasted to *Tonight Show* host Jay Leno in 1997. For anyone else, that would be quite an impressive record. However, Walken has also admitted that he only uses his car to drive up to the corner store to buy the Sunday paper. His reluctance to get behind the wheel traces back to his **childhood**, when a teenage Walken delivered birthday cakes and other delicacies for his family's bakery business. He was always terrified of jeopardizing his cargo with a careless turn or sudden stop and has driven with extreme caution ever since.

Walken's reluctance to go fast borders on the phobic—especially when he's in Los Angeles. "I'm afraid of speeding cars," he says. "I'm afraid of accidents. I'm afraid of disease. I'm very nervous getting on the L.A. freeways with a driver. They drive so fast that if something were to happen you'd be creamed. The 50-mile-per-hour limit was very sensible." (Interestingly enough, Walken experiences traumatic automobile crashes in a number of films, including *The Anderson Tapes* and *The Dead Zone*, and his character in *Annie Hall* contemplates suicide by driving into oncoming traffic.)

WALKEN DIALS UP SOME DANGER AS A TV PRODUCER
IN TONY SCOTT'S FRENETIC *DOMINO*.

Occasionally, Walken's nervous driving has caused him problems with other motorists. People often scream at him and blow their horns as they drive by. One man repeatedly called him a "loser" after he let several cars pass in front of him. In an interview with David Letterman in 2005, Walken told of an even stranger incident when a man he took to be a **police** officer pulled him over on the highway. When the man walked over to Walken's driver's side window, the actor noticed he wasn't wearing a uniform. "I said 'Are you a policeman?' And he said 'No.' There was an awkward moment . . . and he just went back to his car and drove away."

For the record, Walken's vehicle of choice is a **black** Cadillac. "I always wanted a Cadillac," he has said. "All my life my father was saying 'Guy's got a Cadillac!' Well, I got one. It's black. Black outside, black inside. It looks like a bullet. A black bullet. I had all the chrome taken off of it. All the chrome, except the bumpers. All the little nitch-notches, the striping—all that stuff, so it's nice." Rob Lowe, who appeared with Walken in Chekhov's *Three Sisters* at the Williamstown Theatre Festival in 1987, describes Walken's Caddy as looking "like a hearse, man, but he loves that car. . . . We'd be taking a break outside, and he'd be sitting in that car with the windows rolled up. Just sitting there. He'd go sit in that car and stare straight ahead. That did a lot to dispel the rumors that he was not of this world."

"Chaos is out there. Everything is going along nice and then someone jumps the lane and you're in a head-on collision. There's nothing you can do about that. Uh, you can do your best. Wear your seat belt. It's a dangerous world."

—Walken, offering advice to fellow motorists

DRUGS

Although he usually cites vodka as the "**drug** of choice" of his youth, Walken has admitted to experimenting with some other mind-altering substances—including **opium** and **LSD**. However, by all indications his drug and alcohol use seems to have curtailed after a self-confessed bottoming out period in the mid to late 1980s. Of his past drug use, Walken says: "It affected me for the better. It's the reason I don't do it anymore and wouldn't even be inclined or tempted. When it stopped being interesting, I stopped being interested in it. It was a relationship. We gave up on each other."

DUCK JOKE

In 1994, Walken told an interviewer for *Face* magazine what he called his favorite joke: "A duck walks into a drugstore and he says to the pharmacist, 'Could I please have some lip gloss?' The pharmacists say, 'Certainly sir. Here you are. Will this be cash or charge?' And the duck says, 'Oh, put it on my bill.'" Walken must really love this joke, as he has repeated it during several subsequent late-night TV talk-show appearances. He also tells the joke in character as Calvin Webber in the 1999 film *Blast from the Past*.

LAND · FITNESS · FOOD · ED GLOSSER: TRIVIAL PSYCHIC
S · FOOD NETWORK · FRUGALITY · EXCESS BAGGAGE
NTAINS OF WAYNE · FITNESS · ENGLAND · FOOD · ENGI
UBLE · $11,00 · THE ETERNAL · FOOD NETWORK · AB
RARA · THE FUNERAL · FRUGALITY · FANS · ENGLAND
ESS BAGGAGE · $11,000 · ENGLAND · FANS · FRUGALITY ·
SSER: TRIVIAL PSYCHIC · FITNESS · FOUNTAINS OF WAYN
FUNERAL · FITNESS · FOOD NETWORK · ABEL FERRAR
1,000 · FOOD NETWORK · ENGINE TROUBLE · FRUGALIT
LAND · FOOD · ABEL FERRARA · THE ETERNAL · FANS
ESS BAGGAGE · ENGLAND · ABEL FERRARA · FITNESS · FOO
WORK · FOOD · FOUNTAINS OF WAYNE · FANS · THE FUNER
1,000 · FRUGALITY · FANS · ED GLOSSER: TRIVIAL PSYCHI
LAND · FOOD · EXCESS BAGGAGE · ABEL FERRAR
OD NETWORK · FOOD · ENGINE TROUBLE · FOUNTAINS ·
NE · FRUGALITY · THE FUNERAL · ABEL FERRARA · TH
RNAL · ED GLOSSER: TRIVIAL PSYCHIC · $11,000 · FITNE
OD NETWORK · FANS · ABEL FERRARA · EXCESS BAGGAG
LAND · FRUGALITY · ENGINE TROUBLE · FRUGALITY
LAND · FANS · ABEL FERRARA · FOOD · FANS · FOOD NETWOI
E FUNERAL · $11,000 · ED GLOSSER: TRIVIAL PSYCHIC · FOO
WORK · ABEL FERRARA · ENGINE TROUBLE · $11,000
LAND · FITNESS · FOOD · ED GLOSSER: TRIVIAL PSYCH
NS · FOOD NETWORK · FRUGALITY · EXCESS BAGGAGE
NTAINS OF WAYNE · FITNESS · ENGLAND · FOOD · ENGI
UBLE · $11,000 · THE ETERNAL · FOOD NETWORK · AB
RARA · THE FUNERAL · FRUGALITY · FANS · ENGLAND
ESS BAGGAGE · $11,000 · ENGLAND · FANS · FRUGALITY

E TO F

ED GLOSSER: TRIVIAL PSYCHIC

Playing off his *Dead Zone* persona, Walken created this amusing *Saturday Night Live* character for his October 24, 1992 appearance on the program. Glosser is an office worker whose ability to foretell the future is limited to the most mundane events imaginable. Sadly, the promising character was never reprised. On second thought, given *SNL*'s tendency to wear out inspired premises through overexposure, maybe that's a good thing.

$11,000

Amount Walken says was the maximum he ever made in one year until he was paid $14,000 for his role in *The Deer Hunter* in 1978.

ENGINE TROUBLE   ★★

Walken supplies the voice of Rusty, a magical toy fire engine who does his part to help rescue workers in New York City on September 11th, in this seventeen-minute short film that aired on the Showtime network on September 9, 2002. *Engine Trouble* was part of Showtime's *Reflections From Ground Zero* series—a collection of shorts and documentaries dealing with the emotional impact of the 2001 terrorist attacks. It features child actress Celine Du Tertre as a little girl from Connecticut who heeds the call of her talking fire truck and finds a way to get him to Manhattan to assist in the rescue effort. As befits the material, Walken delivers a subdued voice-over performance that is a long way from his over-the-top *Antz* portrayal four years earlier.

ENGLAND

Walken has made several films on location in Great Britain, as well as a memorable 1993 guest appearance on Jonathan Ross's *Saturday Zoo*, where he recited *The Three Little Pigs*. Yet he admits to feeling "very nervous" whenever he stays there. The flow of traffic seems to throw him off. "I'm always looking the wrong way," he says. "Even stepping off the curb, I'm always looking the wrong way. I'm very scared. I walk out of the hotel and think, 'Look that way; look that way,' and I'll do that twenty times, and then I'll get something on my mind and I'll forget it. Not only that, but they drive very fast there."

See also **Driving**.

ENVY   ★

The Dreamworks logo on a film is usually a mark, if not of quality, at least of honest effort. But this agonizingly unfunny comedy may have done irreparable damage to the company's reputation for decades to come. *Envy* is arguably one of the worst major studio comedies in movie history. The *Boston Globe* called it "the multiplex equivalent of an industrial spill." Ben Stiller "stars"—if that word can be applied here—as Tim Dingman, a corporate drone at a suburban sandpaper factory who gets a bad case of the covets after his friend Nick (Jack Black) hits the jackpot with an invention that makes dog feces disappear. (The entirely logical question, "Where does the dog poop go?"—which the characters themselves ask at one point—is never answered.) In the most irritating supporting performance of his career, Walken plays "the J-Man," an insane drifter who inexplicably becomes Stiller's personal guru. Wearing a stringy, ashen wig and a Salvation Army wardrobe, Walken looks indistinguishable from the mad movie director he played in 2001's *America's Sweethearts*. He mugs, raves on about pretzel making, and does everything short of barking at the moon, but even his manic hamming cannot infuse this ghastly farce with any life. *Envy* is so bad it lay curdling on a studio shelf for two years before being released in 2004. Only the success of Jack Black's 2003 film *School of Rock* saved this turkey from the straight-to-video fate it so richly deserved. Even the makers of *Envy* disowned it. Both Black and Dreamworks chief Jeffrey Katzenberg personally apologized for the film during a press conference at the 2004 Cannes Film Festival.

> *"Screw Robin Hood. Screw the Merry Men, you stinko pinko."*
>
> —The J-Man, a Jeffrey Lebowski wannabe, uttering some of the scintillating dialogue that makes *Envy* one of cinema history's most appalling misfires

ETERNAL, THE   ★★

Walken is grossly miscast—but amusing nonetheless—in this Z-grade 1998 horror movie, released in theaters under the title *Trance*. The video title is a more accurate description of the content. The fetching Alison Elliott stars as Nora, an Irish expatriate turned American alcoholic who travels back to the Emerald Isle with her foppish husband (Jared Harris) on a trip to see her old relatives. Walken plays "Uncle Bill" Ferriter, an eccentric Irish landowner. You know he's a loon because he wears tinted octagonal eyeglasses and speaks in an on-again, off-again brogue. He also keeps a two thousand-year-old Druid mummy hidden in his basement. The mummy comes to life, slits Walken's throat, and saws off his head in a bathtub. Walken is out of the movie about one third of the way in, at which point it goes totally downhill. There are plot holes galore, and the main characters are unbelievably stupid, even by horror movie standards. (One suggests popping a Quaalude and getting drunk, even as the evil Druid is bearing down on them.) Still, if you want to see what Walken does with a role that, thirty years before, would have probably gone to Vincent Price, it's worth checking out on video.

See also **Zombie Movies.**

EXCESS BAGGAGE   ★★

In 1997, Walken made two films involving staged kidnappings. Although *Excess Baggage* is a better movie than the lackluster *Suicide Kings*, Walken's part is not nearly as interesting, so take your pick. Alicia Silverstone, fresh off her starmaking turn in *Clueless*, plays a rich teenager who fakes her own abduction to win the attention of her moneybags father. Walken plays "Uncle Ray," the fearsome family fixer whom Daddy sends out to find her. He could play this role in his sleep, but it's still fun to watch him, especially when he tosses a burly diner patron out a second floor window. In a rare case where somebody else steals a movie that Walken is in, Benicio del Toro hijacks the action as a shambling, slow-witted car thief.

> *"Am I such a bad guy? Have I hurt you? Have I shot you? In the groin?"*

—Uncle Ray Perkins, trying to convince Benicio del Toro of his good intentions, in 1997's *Excess Baggage*

FANS

While he's known to be a very private person, Walken enjoys the public recognition that comes with movie star status. He claims to know when other people are checking him out—even if they don't say anything—and is disappointed when no one calls him by name. "If I walk down the street and nothing happens . . . I get sad. And, then, you know, like a miracle, an angel, somebody will say, 'Hey, Chris!' And then I go, 'Ah! Well, it's okay.'"

Like all celebrities, Walken has his share of unhinged fans. He once told Roger Ebert he's constantly being stopped on the street, not by people who recognize him from his films, but by people who think they might have served time with him in prison. One man wrote Walken a letter asking for a $57,000 loan. "He was very specific about the amount," Walken says. "He also sent along a contract in which he laid out how much he'd pay me back each year. I thought, 'Does this guy expect a check or what?'"

For the most part, however, the deranged stalkers keep their distance. "That must be the advantage to having an intimidating persona," Walken says. "I don't get the crazies coming up to me. People are usually friendly."

FERRARA, ABEL

The maverick New York–based director of *King of New York*, *The Addiction*, *The Funeral*, and *New Rose Hotel* is one of Walken's regular collaborators and kindred spirits—even though they live totally divergent lifestyles. "It's odd that we get together at all," says Walken. "He lives downtown, very much enmeshed in the life of the city. I live in Connecticut. I live out in the country. I don't particularly like to go to the city. He stays up all night and goes to bed in the daytime. I like to get up early and go to bed early. It's really odd that we ever got together." The exceedingly cautious Walken is also irked by Ferrara's reckless **driving**, which typically results in the director incurring speeding tickets on his way to visit Walken in Connecticut. "One time, he got three tickets. He shouldn't do that, I always tell him." And when Walken drops by Ferrara's home turf in Manhattan to do a little live theater, his friend invariably ducks out at the intermission. "Every time I'm in a play, he calls and says, 'You gotta get me tickets,' so of course I get them, and he has yet to stay to the end of a performance. I'll say, 'Abel, I'm very hurt. I got you these tickets and I saw you sitting there, and then in the second act, you were gone.' And he'll say, 'I'm sorry, I just couldn't take it.'"

For all their differences, Walken has done some of his finest work under Ferrara's direction. His performance in *King of New York* ranks among the strongest of his career. The pair's Oscar and Felix dynamic must be mutually beneficial, since Ferrara keeps hiring his opposite number. A DIY spirit unites the two. Says Walken: "He does it his own way and I really admire that."

FITNESS

"I'm sort of a closet health fiend," Walken has admitted. Keeping his body in shape is important to him. "Actors, you know, that's all they got," he once said, pointing to his torso. "This is it. This is the factory."

Still, the industry provides myriad inducements for actors to go off their diets. The craft service table is usually the place where the battle of the bulge is won or lost. "Buffets are very dangerous," Walken has said. "A lot of actors I know gain fifteen pounds when they make a movie." Downtime on the set is another pitfall. "There's a lot of sitting around on movie sets and actors are always sitting on their chairs and talking about **food**. It may be because they're on a diet and thinking about it a lot. It's true that the camera is very cruel. It makes you look heavier than you are. And movie food is generally very good, because they have to make sure the technicians are happy. They like a nice big lunch with dessert. It's tempting." After a film is released, premiere parties provide yet another opportunity for cast members to pork up. "Sometimes I go to these movie events, and there'll be a buffet with very good food. You'll see all these important, wealthy people standing on line getting huge plates of it. They don't need it. But psychologically, I guess it's some primitive thing. Somebody's got to eat it."

To stay in shape and keep his "factory" running smoothly, Walken exercises regularly and watches his diet. The result is a cardio profile that would be the envy of most men his age. "My cholesterol is good," he says. "Every time I go to the doctor, he swoons in ecstasy over my blood pressure. I've got some incredible blood pressure." Whatever he's doing, it must be working. Appearing on *Live with*

Regis and Kelly in 2006, Walken proudly wore the same grey sports jacket he wore in *King of New York* sixteen years earlier.

FOOD

Sensible food choices are an important part of Walken's **fitness** plan. In the mornings, he consumes only juice and, occasionally, a piece of fruit. Otherwise, he keeps his refrigerator fairly empty, buys things only as he needs them, and eats only one meal a day, typically around seven o'clock, after the sun goes down. "Eating makes me sleepy," he has said. When he does eat, he adheres to the heart-healthy Mediterranean diet: lots of fruits and vegetables, olive oil in place of butter, plenty of fish, and red wine. As for dessert, he prefers not to indulge. "I eat sweets very rarely," he says. "I don't eat **sugar** . . . When I have coffee, I put molasses in it. It's very good. When I go to a restaurant, people always have dessert, and I always skip it. I might have some cheese or something like that." Actor and Walken impressionist Jay Mohr recalls some of his costar's odd eating habits on the set of *Suicide Kings* in 1997: "He eats the strangest food of anyone I've ever met. He would have a cup of something that looked like chicken soup, and I'd ask him what it was. He'd say, 'Scallops and parsley. And I wash it down with castor oil.' He never had anything simple like a sandwich."

Walken's diet was not always so lean. As a child, his mother served up the "peasant" food of her Scottish heritage: "Things that I never see anymore, like oxtails . . . things like the linings of things." And his father preferred rich German food. "He used to drink sauerkraut juice. . . . this incredibly high-cholesterol stuff. All those big sausages." Not to mention beer, knockwurst, and headcheese, "which is basically these big chunks of fat in gelatin and made into a loaf. It's like eating solid fat." Working in the family bakery also provided ample opportunity for unhealthy snacking. "Every day in the house there was cake, cookies, chocolate cream pies," Walken recalls. "Every week, the cleaning lady would take home a huge bag of stuff. . . . I used to make these big vats of melted chocolate. The smell of sugar in that quantity is overwhelming. It's almost too much."

Somehow Walken and his two brothers managed to make it into adulthood alive—and skinny. "When I was a kid I was really like a pencil," Walken says. "I'd be on the road and I'd eat two pizzas and a six-pack of beer and watch television and then I'd go to bed and I never gained a pound." In his mid-forties, his metabolism slowed and his diet changed. During a July 2007 appearance on *Late Night with Conan O'Brien*, Walken identified spaghetti and ice cream as two of his favorite foods—and the ones he must avoid if he's to keep his weight under control. French, Mexican, and Japanese cuisines also rank among his favorites. His pet peeve is American fast food. "I can't believe the things people eat. Particulary in this country," he says. "The way we eat is just unbelievable. I wish this whole country would eat better."

> *"I was in Japan once, and I said to the people I was with, you know, 'I love Japanese food, so I would like to have some real authentic Japanese food.' And they took me to this restaurant and gave me a bowl of what looked like some pasta. I looked at it. There were all these little eyes, and the whole thing was moving. I think they were little white eels. I did have some of it to be polite. That was tough. I had to take it down with some beer."*
>
> —Walken, describing one of his most unusual food experiences, to the *New York Observer* in 2000

FOOD NETWORK

As a Julia Child fan, **cooking** show aficionado, and would-be cooking show host, Walken should be right smack in the middle of the target demographic for the basic cable **food** channel. But he bailed out on what some have called "The Emeril Network" long ago, due to its overreliance on ads. "Every time you turn on the Food Network, the guy says, 'I'm going to put this in the oven, and when we come right back. . . . ' The commercials are ridiculous," Walken gripes. "I used to watch it all of the time, but now, I swear, for a half-hour show, there must be twenty minutes of commercials!"

FOUNTAINS OF WAYNE

This New York-area power pop band is one of many to name-drop Walken in one of its songs, with the 2003 tune "Hackensack" off its critically acclaimed LP *Welcome Interstate Managers*. Frontman Chris Collingwood has named Walken and John Lennon as his heroes. "Both are geniuses in their own right and I think a lot about each of them when I'm writing my songs."

FRUGALITY

What's the key to Walken's financial success? Never buying anything on credit. "All my life, even when I didn't have any money I never owed anybody any money because I always made a point of that. I never owned anything that I had to borrow to pay for and if I couldn't eat in restaurants I cooked my own food. I always made sure that I never owed anybody money. Even now, if I buy something, I pay for it. I never have mortgages or down payments or any of that."

FUNERAL, THE   ★★★

Walken shines as a logorrheic, philosophizing mobster in this characteristically idiosyncratic gangster movie from director **Abel Ferrara**. The 1996 film also stars Chris Penn and Vincent Gallo as Walken's younger brothers, Anabella Sciorra as his wife, and Benicio Del Toro as a rival racketeer. Set in Depression-era New York City, the gloomy, flashback-laden film tells the story of the violent Tempio family as it deals with the aftermath of the murder of one of its members. Walken plays Ray Tempio, the most contemplative and level-headed of the siblings, who ruminates mordantly on the nature of sin, even as he plots revenge against the man who killed his brother. "We should be taking over the Ford Motor Company instead of shooting each other," he muses at one point. Like most **Abel Ferrara** movies, *The Funeral* is slow, moody, and larded with philosophical insights that don't always flow naturally out of the mouths of the characters. It's not for every taste, but the performances are arresting. Walken called it "a different type of gangster movie. Nobody's particularly sexy or intelligent or romantic or brave or resourceful. There's nothing particularly glamorous about these particular gangsters, which is probably more like the truth."

> *"If I do something wrong, it's because God did not give me the grace to do what's right."*
>
> —Ray Tempio, riffing on the Roman Catholic conception of sin,
> in 1996's *The Funeral*

G TO H

GARLAND, JUDY

Walken danced with this Hollywood icon at her daughter Liza Minnelli's sweet sixteen party in 1962. "She was beautiful. Very sexy, actually," he said of Garland. Walken and Minnelli would soon take the stage together in an off-Broadway production of *Best Foot Forward*.

GIGLI   ★

Mercifully, Walken has only one scene in this 2003 cinematic disaster, whose title has become international shorthand for "dreadful." It's been said that Walken is often the best thing in many bad movies, but neither he nor Al Pacino can resuscitate the corpse of this lifeless mob comedy, which has real-life couple Ben Affleck and Jennifer Lopez playing mismatched underworld soldiers who abduct and belittle a retarded child. A bored-looking Walken plays Detective Stanley Jacobellis in a deadly performance that earned him his second 2003 Razzie Award nomination (the other was for *Kangaroo Jack*). His lone scene consists of him stalking around Affleck's bungalow ranting about Marie Callender's pies. Needless to say, this monologue won't go down in cinema history alongside his *Pulp Fiction* speech or the Sicilian scene from *True Romance*.

Walken was filming *The Stepford Wives* when *Gigli* befouled America's movie screens in August 2003, so he never got to sample his handiwork. "I've never seen it," he has admitted. "It came and went so quickly." He remembers being in his makeup trailer when someone came in with the first batch of newspaper reviews. The ferocity of the negative notices astonished Walken, who never read the full script and couldn't believe it had all gone so horribly wrong.

"I thought it was gonna be good."

—Walken, attempting to explain his participation in one of the worst films
of all time, 2003's *Gigli*

GOLF

Golf may be one of the world's fastest-growing sports, but Walken remains immune to its charms, declaring: "Ugh. Once in a while I come across it on TV and I feel like an alien watching this thing. I don't know what's going on. I hear it's supposed to be really hard, though."

GRAUMAN'S CHINESE THEATRE

Talk about Christopher Walken impressions. On October 11, 2004, the actor left his handprints and footprints in the wet cement outside the world famous Grauman's Chinese Theater in Hollywood. Calling the ceremony "a big day for me," Walken was thrilled to be honored alongside so many of his Hollywood heroes. "I grew up after the Second World War. I've got that stuff imprinted in my brain—the old days, the flashbulbs going off, the people putting their hands in the cement. My family was always fascinated by the movies, so the whole thing's not only an honor, it's a nostalgic thrill."

GROHL, DAVE

The Foo Fighters frontman and former drummer for Nirvana has stated publicly that he wants Walken to play him in a TV miniseries based on his life story. "I'd like Christopher Walken to play me," the rocker told *Rolling Stone*. "Since Chris Walken always plays himself, you can just imagine what it would sound like."

GUIDING LIGHT

Walken and his brother **Glenn** shared the role of the young Mike Bauer on this long-running daytime soap opera from 1954 to 1956. **Christopher** (then known as **Ronnie**) played the role on **television**, while Glenn appeared in the radio version. When Glenn was tied up with other projects, Ronnie filled in for him on the radio show as well.

GUNS

From the Russian roulette finale in *The Deer Hunter* to the sudden, violent shootings that punctuate key scenes in *At Close Range*, *King of New York*, and *True Romance*, gunplay has been an important part of Walken's on-screen persona. Yet when he's away from the camera he professes to detest firearms and prefers not to even point a prop gun at a fellow actor. "I don't even like holding them," Walken once told *Entertainment Weekly*. "Whenever I hold a gun, I want to get it out of my hand as quick as possible."

> *"The whole world would be a lot better off if we melted down every gun."*
>
> —Walken, on his distaste for firearms

HAIR

"I think it's one of my best features," Walken has said of his luxurious, gravity-defying head of hair. "I'm pleased with my hair. I've got great hair." A point of special pride for him has been his ability to stave off baldness, the bane of every male performer. "Most actors, when they watch themselves over the years, they see their hairline go back, but I've been very consistent about that. This is the real thing." Understandably, Walken has always been very protective of his hair, which, as he once observed "was famous before I was." Perhaps he was referring to his idol **Elvis Presley**, after whom he reportedly models his distinctive mane. "The minute I saw him, I started combing my hair that way." He's stuck with the same style ever since, with slight variations to accommodate the parts he plays or shifting trends. In the 1960s, Walken let his hair grow longer, all the way down his back at one point, but, as he points out, "It was still sort of like Elvis with long hair. It was big hair, tall hair. It went up and it went down."

In addition, Walken has long harbored a distaste for hats, preferring not to wear them, as he says, "because the hair was more important." So what's his secret? As a young man, Walken received hair care tips from a somewhat unlikely source—*Psycho* star Anthony Perkins. "He had a great head of hair," Walken told *Playboy* in 1997. "He said the reason men go bald, aside from genes, is that as they get older, the scalp gets tight, the blood gets cut off and the follicles die, particularly with stress. He knew a lot about it." Perkins instructed Walken to ensure proper blood flow by pulling his entire scalp forward by hand and yanking it around for five minutes a day. "I've done it every morning since," Walken reports. "I heard that Kennedy, when he was in the White House, had somebody come in every day and do it for him. He had a great head of hair." Walken gives movie audiences a glimpse of this arcane process in the 1989 film *Communion*, in which his character, Whitley Strieber, vigorously tugs on his mane.

THE HAIR UP THERE

Here are a few select quotes from Walken on one of his favorite subjects: his hair.

"I have had bad haircuts. . . . People who do hair are very temperamental, really. Sometimes you can find a perfectly good hairdresser who's simply having a nervous breakdown that day and gives you a terrible haircut. This has happened to me. It's like fate. It shouldn't have happened but it did and you can't do anything."

"My hair is famous. But even before I was famous, people were talking about my hair, complimenting it, criticizing it, commenting on it, all my life. When I was a kid the other kids used to talk about my hair."

"There's a theory that my hair grows right out of my brain."

"They say that men lose their hair because over the years the skin on the scalp tightens, the blood gets cut off, and the hair dies, like grass, so the thing is to keep the scalp loose by pulling on it."

"It's just a force of nature. It's like animals with the colored feather and tails. If I had a tail, I wouldn't need the hair."

HAIRSPRAY   ★★★

Walken delivers a spirited performance as a chubby-chasing Baltimore novelty shop owner in this 2007 big-screen adaptation of the Tony Award–winning Broadway musical. Based on John Waters's 1988 comedy of the same name, *Hairspray* chronicles the exploits of plus-sized 1960s teen Tracy Turnblad (Nikki Blonsky) who leads a campaign to integrate the local **television** dance program. As Wilbur Turnblad, Tracy's father and the proprietor of the Hardy Har Hut in downtown Baltimore, Walken steps into shoes that were filled on Broadway by such industry giants as Jerry "the Beaver" Mathers and *Too Close for Comfort*'s Jim J. Bullock. He replaced Billy Crystal and Jim Broadbent, the original choices for Wilbur, on the suggestion of costar John Travolta. Travolta plays Edna Turnblad, Wilbur's gargantuan wife, in a fat suit and drag that became the focal point of promotion of the film. Walken himself briefly appears in drag at the end of the movie. For the most part, however, he confines himself to light-up bow ties, oversized novelty wigs, and other accoutrements suitable for a Kennedy–era gag gift purveyor.

HAPPY HOMEOWNERS WALKEN AND JOHN TRAVOLTA BOOGIE THROUGH THEIR BALTIMORE BACKYARD IN THE MUSICAL VERSION OF JOHN WATERS' *HAIRSPRAY*.

Walken and Travolta have one show-stopping number together, the romantic *pas de deux* "You're Timeless to Me." Although neither man's singing voice will make anyone forget Gordon MacRae, it's a surprisingly sweet, effective duet. And it was a triumph of engineering, according to Walken. Extensive rehearsals were required, due to the cumbersome nature of Travolta's fat suit. "This was a huge thing, this costume. And he was in high heels. It was like carrying a mattress. He had to be very strong underneath that. When I saw him in it, I was awe struck. But a few minutes later, when I looked at him again, it was just John under there. I never thought of him as Edna. I just thought of us as Chris and John."

> *"It actually made me think I never get the girl and the first time I do get the girl, it's John Travolta!"*
>
> —Walken, on the mixed blessings of his role as Wilbur Turnblad in *Hairspray*

HAMLET

In 1982, Walken played **Shakespeare**'s tragic Dane at the American Shakespeare Theater in Stratford, Connecticut. It was an ill-starred production that *New York Times* theater critic Mel Gussow called "as close to a travesty of *Hamlet* as I have seen." The curious cast included Fred Gwynne—TV's Herman Munster—as Claudius and *All About Eve*'s Anne Baxter as Gertrude. Both Walken's performance and the experimental staging were widely panned. Even the leading man disowned the project. The production, Walken told the *New York Times*, "took place on Mars or something—the costumes were very strange, it was a very strange thing . . . it was what they call a concept production. I was not happy with it."

HAMLISCH, MARVIN

The renowned film score composer was a classmate of Walken's at the Professional Children's School. Walken, the famed music man would later recall, "was the most handsome devil at school. Because of his looks, he was cast in a lot of our shows.   I particularly remember him doing a number called 'All Dressed Up and No Place to Go.' He was terrific, but no one expected him to become a serious actor. We thought he'd probably end up a model, or maybe in a **musical** comedy."

HAN SOLO

Walken was George Lucas' second choice for the part of the brash pilot of the *Millennium Falcon* in the 1977 sci-fi classic *Star Wars*. In fact, he did a screen test for Lucas in an apartment on Manhattan's Upper West Side, with Jodie Foster playing Princess Leia. ("She was very young. She was just wonderful. Just brilliant," Walken remembers.) Nick Nolte was also considered for the part, which eventually went to Harrison Ford and helped make him a worldwide superstar. **Kevin Spacey** performed a spirited impression of Walken auditioning for the role of Han Solo during a January 1997 appearance on *Saturday Night Live*.

> *"I don't even know that I knew it was called* Star Wars. *I'm sure I was terrible."*
>
> —Walken, on his screen test for the role of Han Solo

HAWAII FIVE-O

Book him, Dan-O. Walken dons his sailor suit to play a U.S. Navy shore patrolman who tries to cover up his involvement in the accidental shooting of his best buddy in "Run, Johnny, Run," a January 1970 episode of this long-running TV **police** drama. Most of Walken's scenes come toward the end of the hour-long show, as Jack Lord's immaculately coiffed Detective Steve McGarrett smokes out Walken's role in the killing. As Patrolman Walt Kramer, Walken gets to do some emoting as he slowly loses his cool under questioning by the unflappable McGarrett. Walken returned to the TV cop genre seven years later, playing a very different kind of criminal—sans sailor suit—in a 1977 episode of *Kojak*.

HEARING

Along with his impeccable hair and consistently perfect blood pressure, Walken also claims to have super hearing powers that are reminiscent of the comic book hero Daredevil.

> *"Almost like a radio, I can tune in on a particular thing and cut out other noises. I can isolate conversations. It can be very interesting and it helps me professionally, listening to two people have a domestic discussion, especially if it's heated and emotional. But it also creates the impression that since I can do it, maybe other people can do it too."*
>
> —Walken, on his super hearing powers

HEAVEN'S GATE   ★

Thirteen years before *Gigli* set a new standard in cinematic futility, Walken starred in the original iconic Hollywood disaster, Michael Cimino's ponderous western epic about labor strife in old Wyoming. That isn't a subject that would make most moviegoers' pulses quicken, but in the hands of a less self-indulgent director this tale about the conflict between a lawman (Kris Kristofferson) and a hired gun for the ranching association (Walken) might have packed more of a dramatic punch. Instead it's one of the most beautiful-to-look-at bad movies of all time. Static and uninvolving, *Heaven's Gate* is woefully thin on narrative. About thirty minutes' worth of plot is stretched out over three-and-a-half hours of screen time. The "action" (such as it is) unfolds with paint-drying torpidity until a bloody final reel in which most of the main characters—including

WALKEN GOES OUT IN A BLAZE OF GLORY IN THE
ILL-FATED WESTERN EPIC *HEAVEN'S GATE*.

Walken's laconic Nate Champion—are violently dispatched. The rest is ornament. There are numerous interminable crowd and battle sequences and seemingly endless shots of immigrants dancing, roller skating, or guffawing for no discernible reason.

The cast labors mightily to hold up under all this decoration, with mixed results. Kris Kristofferson brings his usual stolid dignity to the lead role of Sheriff Jim Averill, although his character remains a cipher throughout. Isabelle Huppert is particularly dreadful as Ella Watson, the frontier madame whose thick French accent is never properly explained. Apparently Cimino was enamored with the Gallic gamine, and lobbied hard to cast her in the picture over studio objections. He shouldn't have bothered. She brings nothing to a role that should have been the linchpin of the film. Sam Waterston gives a moustache-twirling performance as the film's principal villain, Frank Canton, the Snidely Whiplash of 1890s Wyoming. Buried under layers of makeup are Brad Dourif as the town apothecary and Richard Masur (of *Rhoda* and *One Day at a Time* fame) as a blithering Irish train conductor. Look fast for Mickey Rourke as one of Walken's gun-toting sidekicks. No doubt all these respected actors were grateful to have their participation in this catastrophe drowned out in the overall din. For all its visual beauty—and Vilmos Zsigmond's cinematography is its main selling point—*Heaven's Gate* has one of the most cacophonous and incomprehensible soundtracks in movie history.

If there is one redeeming factor about *Heaven's Gate*, from a Walken watcher's perspective, it is Nate Champion's death scene. Holed up in his cabin redoubt, the gunman is set upon by Sam Waterston and his mercenary army. The cabin is set on fire with Champion trapped inside. After dashing off a farewell letter to his beloved Ella, he charges out of the burning building with **guns** blazing. He dies in the ensuing hail of gunshots, but not before showing evidence of an uncanny ability to absorb hot lead that would have made Sonny Corleone jealous. Aside from that blaze of glory, however, Walken's work here is decidedly sub-par—especially coming hot on the heels of his Academy Award-winning performance in *The Deer Hunter*. He literally looks sleepy throughout, even in his death scene. That may have been a consequence of the interminable shooting schedule, which had the cast held virtual hostage in inhospitable Montana locations while Cimino went way off schedule and over budget.

Heaven's Gate premiered in New York on November 19, 1980 and was mercilessly savaged by critics. In a devastating review, Vincent Canby of the *New York Times* compared the film to "a forced four-hour walking tour of one's own living room." Even the recent Oscar winner received his fair share of abuse. "Walken flits in and out of the picture as if he's looking for another game of Russian roulette," cracked the *Boston Globe*. A bullet in the head would have felt like a relief for Michael Cimino, who bore the brunt of the public backlash. Dubbed "Cimino's Folly," *Heaven's Gate* tanked at the box office, and the director was branded a megalomaniac. Despite attempts to cut the film to appease his critics and panicking studio executives, Cimino never regained his stature in Hollywood again.

So what went wrong, from Walken's perspective? A combination of high expectations and some serious production snafus. Anticipation built for Cimino's next picture from the moment *The Deer Hunter* was released. Unrealistic buzz led to inevitable disappointment. "I think that it would not have been so big a deal if people hadn't talked about it so much beforehand," Walken said later. "There were very big expectations and it's better to be modest." The long, arduous Montana shoot also took a toll on the actors. "The locations were so pristine and special that it required four hours of driving to get there. So half the day was used up getting back to the locations by bus or truck over these rough unpaved roads. So the shooting ran eight months"—twice as long as it was supposed to take. The results were visible on screen. "You look at that movie and you can see in certain scenes that the actors, including myself, have been there so long doing the same thing that they don't even know where they are. There is a look on faces in that movie that's, 'Where?' 'Who?' 'Was I born in Montana?' 'Am I ever going home?' And because it was not shot in sequence, you see some scenes toward the end of the movie that were shot in the beginning and everybody is full of juice, and then it's ten minutes later and the actors are different weights, shapes, and they have that 'Where am I?' look." For all the adversity, however, Walken still describes the *Heaven's Gate* experience as "one of the best times I ever had." Certainly at the time he was making it, he and his costars had no idea they were taking part in one of the greatest debacles in movie history. "We all thought we were in *Gone With the Wind*," Walken has said.

"You just shut your big mouth, shitpoke!"

—Nate Champion, telling a fellow mercenary what to do with his pie hole,
in 1980's *Heaven's Gate*

THE CRITICS SPEAK

A selection of reviewer comments on Heaven's Gate:

"The most scandalous cinematic waste I have ever seen."
—Roger Ebert, *Chicago Sun-Times*

"The most spectacular, certainly the most expensive, catastrophe in the annals of the American screen."
—Robert Hatch, the *Nation*

"So ponderous that it fails to work at almost every level."
—*Variety*

"Nothing in the movie works properly . . . . a ship that
slides straight to the bottom at its christening . . . . an
unqualified disaster."
—Vincent Canby, the *New York Times*

HIGH SPIRITS

In one of his earliest Broadway appearances, Walken joined the
chorus of this **musical** version of **Noel Coward**'s *Blithe Spirit* in
1964. His role consisted of standing in the wings and pushing the
show's star, Beatrice Lillie, onstage on a bicycle. "One night she suddenly turned to me and said, 'Oh, hello, you must be the new boy!'
To this day, I don't know if she was kidding or was daffy and really
didn't know I'd been pushing her bike for over five months." *High
Spirits* also provided Walken with insight into the grueling life of a
Broadway chorus boy—a fate he would soon swear off in favor of
dramatic roles. "The guy next to me had a son my age," Walken
recalls. "I kept thinking, 'Boy I hope that I don't have to live hand to
mouth when I'm forty-five.' He seemed happy, but he was dumb. If
he'd been smart, he wouldn't have settled for such a hard way of life."

HIM

Elvis Presley is Walken's hero, so it's only fitting that Presley should
be the subject of the actor's playwriting debut. *Him* enjoyed a brief
run off-Broadway in 1994, with Walken himself playing the part of
Elvis. Originally called *Milk Cow Boogie* (after the title of one of Elvis'
songs), *Him* casts a jaundiced eye on the cult of celebrity as epito-
mized by The King of Rock 'n' Roll, who in Walken's rendering is

dead and well and living in limbo with his twin brother Jesse.

The idea came to Walken during a break in filming *Batman Returns*. He was browsing the tabloids in the supermarket one day when he saw a magazine with a picture depicting Elvis as a middle-aged woman in an angora sweater "with great big knockers." The article claimed The King wasn't really dead; he'd just undergone a sex change operation and was working as a waitress at a diner in Morocco. Inspired, Walken decided to dramatize the concept. "I accumulated a huge amount of these stories, I gathered the information, weird stuff, and I used it to write a play." The theme, as Walken put it, was "Elvis is still with us. He's older. He's his own age. He's lost a lot of weight. He's just been away. He's doing very well." If you call being married to a fat, alcoholic truck driver and looking like Christopher Walken in drag "doing well," that is.

The critics weren't exactly all shook up by Walken's playwriting debut. The *New York Times*'s Vincent Canby called *Him* "woozily conceived" and "cluttered with murky thoughts expressed in windy speeches, illustrated by anecdotes that have no point." Walken himself conceded his heart wasn't always in it on a nightly basis. "It was the hardest thing I ever did, because it wasn't very good. It was very, very whimsical. It really depended on what kind of mood I was in when I did it. If I was feeling silly enough, and brave enough, outrageous enough, it usually worked okay. That was usually on a weekend. Again, it had to do with the audience. There was something very silly about it that I think the audience had to share with you."

> *"I did it eight times a week, and six times it was funny and twice it wasn't."*

—Walken, on his play *Him*, about the troubled "**afterlife**" of Elvis Presley

HOFSTRA UNIVERSITY

Walken attended this Long Island college for less than one year. "It wasn't Harvard," he has said dismissively of the Hempstead, NY institution, which he literally walked out of on a whim. "I was sitting in psychology class, and it was spring. I was looking out the window, and I just got up and left. Never had a second thought about it either."

> *"It was probably for the best, because I knew I was never going to be a rocket scientist."*
>
> —Walken, on his decision to drop out of college

HOLMES, JOHN

In the 1990s, Walken worked diligently on a screenplay based on the life and legend of adult film star Johnny "Wadd" Holmes. The prodigiously endowed actor, whom Walken has called "the **Elvis** of porn," died of AIDS in 1988. His spectacular rise and tragic fall eventually became the inspiration for the 1997 film *Boogie Nights*. Walken's unproduced script would have been more of a straight biopic.

The idea for a John Holmes movie came to Walken while he was shooting *King of New York* in 1990. "**Abel Ferrara** and I were sitting at four A.M. and this guy handed me a *Village Voice* article about John Holmes. . . . He was this simple guy whose father was abusive, and he came to L.A. to work as a handyman, and he never realized he had this great gift. . . . I told his story in my script but I gave it a happy ending, a dream thing where he's very sick and stumbling along and goes back to his apartment and he has this fantasy life with his Donna Reed wife and kids and dog."

Likening Holmes to Vincent Van Gogh and other tormented

artists, Walken planned to make a movie about "an ordinary guy, a very nice man, an adult who was just kind of discovered. He had this, um, big talent but he just took it for granted." His initial plan was to play the role of Holmes himself, with his friend Ferrara in the director's chair. At one point, Ferrara described Walken as "obsessed with Holmes," apparently because he identified with the pressures of fame that drove the porn star into drug addiction and death. "He relates to all this because that's what thirty-three years in show business is like."

Unfortunately, no studio would touch Walken's Holmes project—or his ten-inch pole. "I had a lot of lunches and a lot of people say they were enthusiastic, but nothing ever happened," Walken reported some years later. Eventually he became too told to play the part convincingly, and the Johnny Wadd biopic died on the vine.

> *"Basically it's about the curse of a great gift.*
> *It's like Mozart."*
>
> —Walken, on his unproduced screenplay about the life and times
> of porn star "Johnny Wadd" Holmes

HOMEBOY   ★★

This gritty 1988 film about a low-rent boxer and his unscrupulous manager had its genesis in the most unlikely of settings—the rugged mountains of northwest Montana. Walken and Mickey Rourke had bonded there on the set of *Heaven's Gate* in 1980. One day during the interminable shoot the two actors got to talking about dinosaurs. Walken related a theory he had read about in a science magazine, which held that dinosaurs didn't really go extinct, but evolved into birds instead. Rourke found the idea fascinating and filed it away for inclusion in a screenplay he was thinking about developing, about a brain-damaged fighter and his corrupt handler. Rourke already envisioned himself and Walken in the two leads. Fast forward to 1988 and *Homeboy*. Rourke, a former Gold Glove boxer, plays Johnny Walker, a borderline retarded pugilist who risks his life and health for one last shot at a big purse. Walken plays Wesley Pendergass, Johnny's lowlife manager, who withholds critical medical information and tries to enlist him in an armed robbery. (Wesley also quotes Aristotle, dresses up as a Hasidic Jew, and performs a soft shoe rendition of the pop standard "Fine and Dandy" in a nightclub setting—all decidedly Walkenesque flourishes.)

The film was heavily improvised, a tactic made all the more necessary by the laconic—almost catatonic—nature of Rourke's character. "It seemed a good idea," Walken said later. "Particularly for my character, because Mickey plays someone who doesn't say much. We're together a lot, and if two people don't say much then you just sit there and look at each other. So I ended up talking nonstop." Among the things Walken's blabbermouth promoter talks about, of course, are flying dinosaurs. "I said to [Mickey], 'Why don't I tell that story about the birds and dinosaurs?' He said, 'Right.' It's completely disconnected from anything going on in the movie, but I think it's one of the best things in the movie. . . . It's real. Here are these two guys who are really kind of victims, talking about the origin and destiny of dinosaurs."

"HOOK"

This 1940 tale by Walter Van Tilburg Clark, best known as the author of the novel *The Ox-Bow Incident*, is one of Walken's favorite short stories. "Hook" takes the point of view of a red-tailed hawk living along the Big Sur coast in California. The story climaxes with Hook's death, a passage that Walken used as the inspiration for Frank White's death scene in *King of New York*.

HORSES

Despite appearing in numerous westerns over the years, Walken is deathly afraid of horses and refuses to ride one. "I'll sit on a horse," he says, "but if it moves, I don't. In the westerns I've done, I get on the horse and somebody else rides off."

When he signed on to play The Hessian Horseman in 1999's *Sleepy Hollow*, Walken informed producers of his equinophobia and requested that they provide him with a mechanical mount for his galloping scenes. Luckily the prop horse used by Elizabeth Taylor in *National Velvet* was still in mothballs, so that's the adorable Piebald you see Walken riding in that picture.

> *"People say that horses are smart animals, but I don't believe it—they do whatever they want."*
>
> —Walken, on his fear of horses

HOUSE OF BLUE LEAVES

Walken garnered kudos for his cameo role as Billy Einhorn, a Queens native turned Hollywood mogul, in the 1986 off-Broadway revival of John Guare's 1971 play. *House of Blue Leaves* eventually moved to Broadway, where it garnered eight Tony nominations, including Best Play. By that time, however, Walken had left the cast to start filming *Deadline* in Tel Aviv. He was replaced by Danny Aiello.

HOWDY DOODY

As a child actor working in New York's Rockefeller Center, Walken plied his trade in the same studio where *Howdy Dowdy* was broadcast. He often got an unvarnished look at the freckle-faced marionette when the cameras were turned off. "I'd see Howdy Doody lying where they'd dump him on a couch," Walken later recalled.

HURLYBURLY

Whenever he takes a stage role, Walken has an escape clause put in his contract that allows him to leave the production before the end of its run to take on a part in a film. "After four months I always start to get ants in my pants," he once explained. Despite receiving terrific notices for his portrayal of Mickey, the cynical casting agent, in the original 1984 Broadway production of David Rabe's blistering Hollywood satire, Walken flew the coop after four months to play **Max** Zorin in the **James Bond** film *A View to a Kill*. He was replaced by Ron Silver. *Hurlyburly* went on to receive four Tony Award nominations, including Best Play. **Kevin Spacey** played the part of Mickey in the 1998 movie version. Of Walken's performance, Frank Rich of the *New York Times* wrote that he "offers what may be his least mannered, most fully ripened comic performance ever."

IJ TO J

ILLUMINATA   ★★

Walken drew on one of his favorite sources of inspiration—**Renzo Cesana's Continental**—to play Umberto Bevalaqua, a foppish gay theater critic, in this 1998 indie feature from actor/director John Turturro. A ribald comedy in the tradition of *Shakespeare in Love*, *Illuminata* follows the members of an early twentieth century theater troupe as they politic, scheme, stab each other in the back, and hop in and out of one another's beds while preparing to put on Turturro's new play. Turturro, who co-wrote the screenplay, gave Walken his choice of parts. Walken naturally gravitated to the most outrageous and over-the-top character in the film. Bevalaqua is a Caravaggio-loving "macaroni queen" who doles out favorable reviews to the male actors who capture his fancy. At one point he performs a seductive striptease for a would-be paramour. To play the part convincingly, Walken slathered on lipstick, used his **Continental** voice, and exploited one of his greatest physical assets: "I had a lot of hair at the time and I just combed it forward." The result is one of the most unique looking creations in Walken's long career. Even if the film sags a bit after a frenetic start, he's hard not to watch whenever he comes on screen.

"I've always been different. My hair grows directly out of my brain."

— Umberto Bevalaqua, explaining what sets him apart from the other flamboyant gay theater critics, in 1998's *Illuminata*

IMPRESSIONS

"My wife says **Kevin Spacey**'s is the best," says Walken of the many actors who do impersonations of his unique vocal style. Kevin Pollak and Jake Gyllenhaal have also won praise for their dead-on Walken impressions. So has *Saturday Night Live* alum Jay Mohr, who got to work with the object of his imitation in the 1997 film *Suicide Kings*

A GLOWERING WALKEN SURVEYS THE ITALIAN THEATER
SCENE IN JOHN TURTURRO'S *ILLUMINATA*.

and added the original twist of having "his" Walken be a television pitchman for Skittles. In recent years, the fever for Walken mimicry has even crossed the Atlantic. British actor Max Beesley reportedly once tried to win over a top New York casting director with his impression of Walken as Nick in *The Deer Hunter*. There was just one problem: unbeknownst to Beesley, the casting director was Walken's wife, **Georgianne**.

"It's interesting that a lot of guys do me," the real Chris Walken once observed. The oft-imitated actor professes not to hear anything odd in his own cadence, and has admitted he is tickled when he suddenly hears "his" voice coming out of someone he knows. "I have a friend who does me on his answering machine so when I call him I talk to myself."

"I don't really know what that comes from.   It doesn't seem to me that I speak in a strange way."

—Walken, on the proliferation of Walken impressionists

IMPROVISATION

Although he's famous for reading his lines in a variety of accents, styles, and cadences, Walken is actually not that prodigious an improviser—unless the nature of the piece calls for it, or the groundwork has been laid through preparation. "Improvising is wonderful," he says. Although he adds

> But, the thing is that you cannot improvise unless you know exactly what you're doing. That's a kind of paradox-ical thing about improvising. Improvisation is wonderful and in fact, in the movies, those are the things that you remember most, little accidents, something happens that's

spontaneous and the camera's rolling and it's wonderful, you know, it's like life. Some actors are very good at it, and I'm good at it too, but only when I know exactly what I'm doing. When I know that, if I have no inspiration whatsoever, when I come and I just feel empty, I have nothing, I know that I can still play the scene.

IRON CHEF

Walken is a huge fan of the original Japanese version of this TV **cooking** competition program, which pits master chefs against one another in a culinary battle centered around a secret ingredient. "I love *Iron Chef*," he has said. "I love that. They dub it, so it's a little bit like a Godzilla movie. The Iron Chef's making seven courses and every one of them contains peaches. Mackerel and peaches. Disgusting, you know. Tofu with peaches. That's a really good show."

JAMAICA

According to David Lancaster, the producer of Walken's 1993 Showtime TV movie *Scam*, Walken is revered by the inhabitants of the Caribbean island nation because of his portrayal of Frank White, the white leader of a black drug gang, in 1990's **King of New York**. Says Lancaster: "In Jamaica, he's a god."

JAMES BOND

Christopher Walken as 007? Apparently bedeviling Roger Moore in *A View to a Kill* and playing sidekick to original Bond, Sean Connery, in *The Anderson Tapes* wasn't enough for him. "I'd love to play a hero," Walken once declared. "I'd love to play James Bond. Nobody's going to ask me to play James Bond." No, Chris, nobody is.

JAMES JOYCE'S *THE DEAD*

Making his first appearance on Broadway in more than fourteen years, Walken received a Tony Award nomination as Best Actor in a **Musical** for his performance as Gabriel Conroy in this 1999 stage adaptation of James Joyce's short story. "Chris, in this role, is a revelation to a lot of people," observed *The Dead*'s writer/director Richard Nelson. "He's a man of great charm, and wit, and grace. People have seen his movies, and they forget this side of him." Of special interest to fans of Walken were the numerous songs he was asked to sing. The show's producers implored him to work with a vocal coach before opening night, but Walken informed them it was too late to improve his "small . . . extremely unpleasant" singing voice.

J. B.

In 1959, Walken made his professional acting debut in this play by Archibald MacLeish at Broadway's ANTA Playhouse. A dramatic reenactment of the Book of Job set in a ramshackle circus, *J. B.* won both the Pulitzer Prize for Drama and a Tony Award for Best Play. Walken's costars in the production included Hollywood Sherlock Holmes Basil Rathbone and James Daly, father of actors Tim and Tyne Daly.

JERRY SPRINGER SHOW

While *Charlie Rose* remains his favorite talk show, Walken professes a perverse fascination with the legendary daytime **television** ringmaster: "I can't keep my eyes off Jerry Springer," he says. "How do they find all these crazy people week after week? It's funny. I like when they ring the bell and everybody charges at each other."

JOE DIRT   ★

Kicking off what would be an unintentional trilogy of godawful

A BEWILDERED WALKEN SLEEPWALKS THROUGH
THE DREADFUL DAVID SPADE COMEDY *JOE DIRT*.

comedies (see *Gigli* and *Kangaroo Jack*), Walken took a supporting role in this lowbrow 2001 feature about a mullet-headed redneck in search of the parents who abandoned him when he was eight. *Saturday Night Live* alum David Spade plays the titular imbecile, who encounters Walken's character, Clem, while working as a janitor in a New Orleans high school. For reasons that are largely unexplained—not to mention totally irrelevant to the plot—Clem is an ex-mobster now living incognito in the witness protection program. Walken does what he can to bring some life to the leaden material he's asked to read. He dances with his mop and issues the occasional maniacal wiseguy pronouncement like "You do that again and I'll stab you in the face with a soldering iron!" Sadly, no amount of Walkenesque capering can save this painfully unfunny potty-mouthed farce, which mercifully put the phenobarbital to David Spade's stillborn movie career. Or did it? Undeterred by the film's disastrous critical and commercial response, *Joe Dirt*'s perpetrator was publicly threatening the world with a sequel as recently as spring 2007.

JULIUS CAESAR   ★★★

"I always wanted to do a toga movie," Walken says of his participation in this 2004 **television** miniseries chronicling the rise and fall of the legendary Roman general. As a lifelong fan of such "sword-and-sandal" epics as *Spartacus* and *Ben Hur*, he got a real kick out of playing Cato the Younger in the well-received telefilm, which was shot on location on the island of Malta. "I play a very nice man, unusually for me," Walken explained. "Actually, he is the nicest person in the film, which is another reason why I took the part," To be fair, his Cato is a bit of a schemer, constantly carping about Caesar (Jeremy Sisto) behind his back. Nevertheless, Walken enjoyed wearing his "comfortable, relaxing" toga—despite a tendency to trip over its folds—and soaking up the Mediterranean sun. In a particularly batty costuming choice, for the first half of the film, Walken is outfitted in a curly toupee that makes him look, as he put it, "like Harpo Marx." About halfway through, he inexplicably stops wearing it. For the balance of the four-hour production, he sports a modern, shoulder-length hairstyle—although no one in Rome seems to notice the change. Did someone open a salon next door to the vomitorium?

See also **Hair.**

JUNGLE

Having had his fill with *The Deer Hunter*, Walken vows never again to reenter the canopy for another exotic location shoot. "I would have to really need money to do another jungle movie," he says. "I'm never going back to the jungle. It's a nightmare. Getting up at night and turning on the light in the bathroom? You see lots of, you know, scary things. I'm never going back."

K to L

KANGAROO JACK   ★

"He stole the money—and he's not giving it back!" screamed the posters for this 2002 feature. That captures the sentiments most moviegoers must have felt toward producer Jerry Bruckheimer upon their exit from the theater.

If you've ever dreamed of hearing Walken's voice coming out of the mouth of a CGI kangaroo, then rent this excruciatingly unfunny comedy intended—one can only hope—for children. Otherwise there's no point in watching this woebegone farce, which has Walken

CRIMELORD SALVATORE "SAL" MAGGIO, WALKEN DISPATCHES TWO IMBECILES A FRUITLESS MISSION TO AUSTRALIA IN THE INANE COMEDY *KANGAROO JACK*.

going through the motions as a Brooklyn mob boss who inexplicably sends his idiot stepson and his clownish best friend to Australia to deliver an envelope filled with cash to an underworld associate. Jerry O'Connell and Anthony Anderson play the two buffoons, who wind up losing the money to the elusive title marsupial. Ads for the film made it seem like the kangaroo could talk and rap, which sadly isn't the case (though it does speak with Walken's voice during a brief dream sequence). Walken's listless performance earned him a Golden Raspberry Award nomination for Worst Supporting Actor.

> *"Everybody loves kangaroos."*
>
> —Walken, explaining his decision to take part in the marsupial misfire *Kangaroo Jack*

KID CHAMPION

Walken won an Obie Award for his performance as a **drug**-addled rock star in this 1975 off-Broadway musical loosely based on the life of Doors frontman Jim Morrison. Music was supplied by frequent Meat Loaf co-conspirator Jim Steinman. "I was a monster," Walken said of his character. "I was the biggest bastard that ever lived, because that guy was the biggest bastard." In fact, he so fully lost himself in his lizardly creation that his own wife looked forward to the end of the play's run. **Georgianne Walken** quickly got her wish, as *Kid Champion* closed after just six weeks of performances. In an otherwise scathing review for the *New York Times*, critic Clive Barnes singled out Walken for praise, crediting his "scorpion whim, petulant good looks, and . . . lazily arrogant manner" with *almost* salvaging his cliché of a character.

KING OF NEW YORK   ★★★★

If Walken's defining role is *The Deer Hunter*'s Nick Chevotarevich, then Frank White, the charismatic crime boss he created for this superb new jack gangster movie from director **Abel Ferrara**, may represent his most quintessentially Walkenesque performance. For starters, it's a lead role, so you get more than one hundred minutes of sustained Walkenness. From the moment Frank White comes on screen—in a legendary opening sequence showing his release from prison—to the memorable final scene when he dies of a gunshot wound in the back seat of a New York City taxi cab in the middle of a traffic jam, Walken dominates this movie as he never has before or since.

Like *Scarface*, a film to which it's often compared, *King of New York* makes an unlikely hero out of a ruthless killer—a cop-murdering, drug-dealing lowlife who tries to buy his way into respectable society by financing hospitals for sick children. Like *Scarface*, the film has attracted a sizable cult following in the hip-hop community. The Notorious B.I.G. (Biggie Smalls) once even christened himself "the black Frank White" in the title character's honor. Although Frank is one of the most pathologically violent characters in the Walken pantheon, the actor was determined to give him a sympathetic airing on screen. "I always thought Frank White was obviously abandoned as a child. He's a little like the boy who was raised by wolves. I thought of him as always with animals, as an animal in fact, a hawk. He was noble but he was predatory. He came up in a very strange way and it left its mark. That's the way I make the bridge between myself, raised in show business, and Frank White." For the crucial final scene, Walken drew inspiration from one of his favorite short stories, "**Hook**" by Walter Van Tilburg Clark. In the story, a red-tailed hawk named Hook has its wing broken by a farmer. "The hawk has to live on the ground for a long time, and the other animals are constantly trying to get at him. But they don't come too close because they're still afraid, and they're not going to come near him until he dies. I thought that's why the **police** won't come near Frank at the end of the film."

There are a lot of other great Walken moments in *King of New York*—from his impromptu dance with Laurence Fishburne and the members of his criminal crew to his shocking, brutal shotgunning of David Caruso's **police** detective. Many of these scenes were almost totally improvised. "Abel and I have a strong understanding of what each other wants," Walken says. "We want the same things. He's a guy who says, I want to make a movie, and I don't know what it's going to be about, but let's make it anyway." A day on the set would typically start with the actors conferring with the director about the general premise of the scene they were about to shoot. "We'd get there in the morning and say, 'Well, what are we gonna do?' And he'd say, 'Well, we got a body in the trunk.'" The dialogue was almost entirely extemporized. In the hands of a less-skilled group of actors, the results could have been painfully stilted, but *King of New York* benefits enormously from its talented cast—including then-up-and-comers Caruso, Wesley Snipes, and Steve Buscemi.

Amazingly, one of the only people not pleased with Walken's work in *King of New York* was Walken himself. "It should have been my best work, but I fucked up," he says. "I felt that I didn't give Frank enough complexity and perspective. You don't see enough anguish in his face and the things that drive him to do what he does. I wish I had another chance to play him because I would have completely altered my performance. . . . Both myself and the director, Abel Ferrara, worked hard at creating a mysterious edge to Frank's personality but we lost his motivation and a sense of where he was coming from. So I'm disappointed by what comes off on the screen."

Its lead actor's reservations aside, *King of New York* remains one of the signature performances of Walken's career. The film also set a template for a slew of violent, stylized crime films to follow in the 1990s—from *Reservoir Dogs* to *New Jack City*. For years, rumors have

WALKEN PLAYS THE DEATH CARD IN ABEL FERRARA'S
BRILLIANT GANGLAND DRAMA *KING OF NEW YORK*.

abounded that **Abel Ferrara** is working on a prequel. Don't count
on Walken being a part of it, however. "I don't know what I'd play,"
Walken told *Premiere* magazine in 2004. "I'm way too old to play
Frank now. Maybe if it was a sequel like *The Godfather*, a few years
on. Or maybe now I could play his father or something."

"I never killed anybody that didn't deserve it."

—Frank White, explaining away his brutal life of crime, in 1990's *King of New York*

WALKEN'S PERFORMANCE AS FRANK WHITE IN *KING OF NEW YORK* IS ONE OF HIS FINEST—AND LEFT A LASTING IMPRESSION ON THE NOTORIOUS B.I.G.

SCARED OF GUNS?

One of the most famous scenes in *King of New York* involves Frank White's intrusion on a card game involving a group of low-level Italian mobsters who have been encroaching on his turf while he was away in the slammer. The scene ends with Walken mowing down the entire room full of mooks—shooting several of them multiple times just for emphasis. It was a sequence that almost didn't come off, according to **Abel Ferrara**:

"The first day we were shooting, we did that scene with the Italians around the table. And Chris says to me, 'I don't like pointing a gun at another actor.' And I was like, 'Oh, man, we've got to shoot a whole movie with **guns** and you're telling me you don't like pointing a gun at another actor?' And then we did the scene and Chris shot that guy five times after he was dead; that wasn't in the script! He says he's afraid of guns, and then you say 'Action' and he became—how do you say it? Very efficient."

K.I.S.S. GUIDE TO CAT CARE

Walken wrote the foreword to this 2001 book by animal behaviorist Steve Duno. Described by the publisher as "the only guide you'll ever need to keep your cat happy and contented," this "keep it simple" handbook to feline husbandry must have appealed to the practical pet owner in Walken. In his foreword, he rhapsodizes about a number of feline characteristics he admires and recounts the last days of his beloved pet **cat**, Pookie.

KISS TOLEDO GOODBYE   ★

"I've made—I think about a hundred movies," Walken told an interviewer for *Details* in 2007. "And there's a good number of them that I've never seen. Never." *Kiss Toledo Goodbye* is almost certainly somewhere on that list. Walken's face is featured prominently on the video box for this tepid mob comedy, but fans shouldn't be fooled. He actually has a rather thankless minor role as **Max**, a hoodlum whose shoes could have been filled by a thousand less talented—and less expensive—actors, with a marginal effect on the quality of the overall product. Truth be told, this 1998 feature is a flavorless sitcom that makes the similar films *Mickey Blue Eyes* and *Analyze This* look like *Goodfellas* by comparison. Michael Rapaport stars as Kevin Gower, a feckless office drone who discovers that his father is a mafia don. When the old man gets whacked, he takes over the family business—with an assist from a glowering Walken. The film's absurd title is never explained.

WALKEN MARKS HIS TERRITORY

Kiss Toledo Goodbye may be one of Walken's more forgettable films, but he approached it with the same intensity he brought to more worthy projects like *The Deer Hunter* and *King of New York*. According to *Toledo* producer Ivana Chubbuck, in her book *The Power of the Actor*:

> With each new set and on every new location, Walken would walk around on the dark set (before the set was lit) touching and generally using the furniture—sitting in a chair, touching items on the coffee table, perusing the books on the book-shelf—until the space was real to him and contained the appropriate history and feelings. He was invoking his place. So when it was time to actually film the scene, there was no distinction—Walken's world and the set were one.

KNIVES
Walken collected knives as a child growing up in Queens, NY.

KOJAK   ★★★
Who loves ya baby? In a rare primetime TV appearance, Walken plays Ben Wiley, a ruthless fur thief who runs afoul of no-nonsense New York City **police** lieutenant Theo Kojak in "Kiss It All Goodbye," a February 1977 episode of this long-running cop show. Series star Telly Savalas also directed the episode, which gave Walken an early opportunity to show off his villainous chops on screen. In the climactic scene, Walken dumps a disabled woman out of her wheelchair before Kojak apprehends him by trapping him inside the revolving door to a Manhattan apartment building. Oddly enough, two years later, Savalas was the presenter who handed Walken his Best Supporting Actor Oscar for *The Deer Hunter* at the 1979 Academy Awards.

LAST EMBRACE   ★★
Director Jonathan Demme channels the spirit of Alfred Hitchcock— and Walken comes along for the ride—in this mildly diverting 1979 thriller, the first feature released after his Oscar-winning turn in *The Deer Hunter*. *Last Embrace* stars Roy Scheider (who, ironically, was originally cast as Michael, the Robert De Niro part, in *The Deer Hunter*) as Harry Hannan, a burnt-out secret agent who finds himself the target of a bizarre murder conspiracy. Walken has a small role as Eckart, Hannan's officious boss at the unnamed spy agency. He wears grossly oversized eyeglasses and what appears to be a false moustache. Janet Margolin and John Glover also appear. The convoluted plot involves white slavery, multiple assassination attempts, and cryptic death threats issued in ancient Aramaic. A climactic confrontation at Niagara Falls shamelessly echoes the Mount Rushmore finale of *North*

by Northwest. Demme had much better luck with his next thriller, 1991's *Silence of the Lambs*. He and Walken worked again on the 1982 **television** film *Who Am I This Time?* for PBS's *American Playhouse*.

LAST MAN STANDING   ★★

"I loved my gangster," Walken has said of his role as Hickey, a ruthless gunman, in this 1996 shoot 'em up loosely based on Akira Kurosawa's *Yojimbo*. "He's the enforcer, the independent guy who's called in to fix things." Bruce Willis is John Smith, the steely-eyed stranger who runs afoul of Hickey and the rest of the Irish mob that runs Jericho, a Prohibition-era ghost town. In a departure from type, Walken's character has relatively little dialogue. He mostly speaks with his tommy **gun**. When he does talk, it's in a craggy, guttural voice that makes him sound like Gabriel from **The Prophecy** with a frog in his throat.

According to producer Arthur Sarkissian, Walken was cast in the part because of his screen presence, not his gangster pedigree. "Willis has an imposing presence, and you have to believe someone like Walken that could stand up to his character." Walken elaborates: "I walk into town, and [Willis] has killed half of my gang. He's a force that has to be reckoned with. A character like that in movies, especially if he's played by someone like Bruce, needs a villain to contend with. It's like that thing about fighters. They say that big fighters know when another big fighter enters the gymnasium. It's true. There's an electricity between our characters when we finally meet face-to-face."

Production on *Last Man Standing* began in early September 1995. Walken arrived fresh from shooting **Abel Ferrara**'s *The Funeral*, where he played a more prolix iteration of a gangland thug. The switch to playing the trigger-happy Hickey must have been refreshing, as Walken seems to have had a lot of fun on the set. "There was an aspect to it that was very much like what I did when I was a kid with my friends," he said in an interview promoting the film. "We

WALKEN BLOWS AWAY ANOTHER ENEMY IN THE DEPRESSION–ERA
SHOOT 'EM UP *LAST MAN STANDING*.

all looked like gangsters from one of my neighborhoods in Queens." The chance to play dress-up on his second straight movie also appealed to him. "You stick a hat on and you feel different," he declared of Hickey's dapper chapeau.

"Hickey was me with a scar on my face."

—Walken, on his role as a disfigured Depression-era gunsel in 1996's *Last Man Standing*

LAST TEMPTATION OF CHRIST, THE

Walken was director Martin Scorsese's first choice to play the role of Jesus in his big-screen adaptation of Nikos Kazantzakis' novel. Scorsese had optioned the novel in the late 1970s, and began discussing the part with Walken some time after his Oscar-winning performance in *The Deer Hunter* made him a household name. "I'd go over to his house and talk about it," Walken later recalled. "I was going to do that and they cancelled it. Then they were going to do it again, and they cancelled it again. By the time they made it, I was gone. But I was with him for some time. Talking and getting ready for the film. It was fascinating. We looked at paintings a lot." With Walken out of the picture, the role of Jesus was offered to Aidan Quinn and eventually to Willem Dafoe, who starred in the finished film in 1988.

LAUGHING MAN, THE

As a child, Walken was a huge fan of this western movie serial. A mysterious cowboy hero reminiscent of *The Lone Ranger*, *The Laughing Man* carried a **knife** with a picture of himself on the handle. His signature move was to enter a saloon full of bad guys and throw the knife into a table, where it would quiver, animating his own cackling image. "And then he would, of course, destroy them all," Walken says.

"I used to come out of cowboy movies talking like a cowboy, even though I was in Queens. And it would take me half a day to get over that."

—Walken, on his childhood fascination with western heroes like *The Laughing Man*

LEAFBLOWERS

Walken has a problem with handheld gardening tools designed to disperse yard debris. "That should be against the law," he rails.

LEE, GYPSY ROSE

Born Rose Louise Hovick, this world-famous burlesque diva—whose memoir served as the basis for the Broadway musical *Gypsy*—handed Walken his high school diploma at the Professional Children's School in 1961. As a child, Walken was friends with Lee's son, Eric.

LEWIS, JERRY

The adenoidal comedy legend is one of Walken's show business heroes. Walken credits his **childhood** appearance on *The Colgate Comedy Hour*, starring Lewis and partner Dean Martin, with inspiring him to pursue a career in show business. Often, when he is shooting a movie, Walken will crack up the crew by performing a take using Lewis' voice. "Or I'll say, right before a take, 'Is it hot in here, or am I crazy?' For some reason it makes people laugh also."

LION IN WINTER, THE

In 1966, Walken won the prestigious Clarence Derwent Award for his performance as King Philip of France in the original Broadway production of this James Goldman play. A tale of palace intrigue set in the court of England's King Henry II, *The Lion in Winter* was adapted for the big screen two years later with future **James Bond** Timothy

Dalton in the Walken role. On stage, however, Walken owned the part from day one. "Chris came in, and he seemed very young, but he had all this presence and authority," Goldman told *Esquire* magazine. "He also had the physical grace and natural dignity to play a seventeen-year-old king. We didn't look any further." Rosemary Harris, who starred as Eleanor of Aquitaine, echoed that sentiment: "I knew from the first day I saw him that Chris was something special," she said.

The Lion in Winter was Walken's big theatrical breakthrough, but it was almost his biggest career disaster. During the show's tryout run in Boston, he obsessed over learning his lines and was so nervous on stage that his hands shook uncontrollably. When a scene called for him to pour wine into a goblet and hand it to someone, he trembled so much he spilled wine all over the stage. It quickly became apparent that Walken was too much of a wreck to continue in the play. One night the show's producer, Eugene Wolsk, took him out to dinner and fired him. Walken pleaded for three more days to get his act together. Wolsk agreed and Walken, faced with the possible end of his dramatic stage career, somehow managed to control his shakes. When the show opened in New York, Walken received excellent notices. Stanley Kauffmann, writing in the *New York Times*, praised his "silky, proud performance." Less than a month later, Walken copped a Derwent—essentially $500 and a trophy—for best performance in a non-featured role. "This showed me things weren't so bad after all," he later remarked.

> *"It wasn't until after I was fifty that I could stand in the wings and look forward to going on stage and not have a sense of dread."*

—Walken, recalling the terrible stage fright that almost cost him his breakthrough role in Broadway's *The Lion in Winter*

LION TAMING

During the summer of 1960, Walken worked as an assistant lion tamer for the Tarryl Jacobs Circus in New York City. His job was to pose as chief lion tamer Tarryl Jacobs' son, complete with boots, jodhpurs, a red jacket, and a whip. Walken's act consisted of entering the cage of a toothless, elderly lion named Sheba, cracking a whip, and exhorting the enfeebled beast to follow his commands. "She always had this look on her face like, 'Oh no. We gotta do this again?'" Walken recalls. "And I'd take the whip and say, 'Up, Sheba! Up!' And she would go 'Uuuuh!' And then drop down and the audience would give me a huge hand."

Walken spent only two months with the circus, which had the run-down, gamey feel of a traveling carnival. One day Walken's brother Glenn dropped by the lion cage for a visit. As they were talking, a lion strolled over and urinated on him. "I don't think he spoke for three days. But that was interesting," Walken says. Although he and Sheba bonded, the aspiring actor came away less than impressed by circus owner and head lion tamer, Tarryl Jacobs. "[He] would take his shirt off; and it was like lions had been chewing on him for twenty-five years," Walken remembers. "He was just shredded all over the place. And that's what he did for a living. I don't know. I guess he wasn't a very good lion tamer."

> *"She was so well-trained. She was like a dog, a big German shepherd."*
>
> —Walken, on his leonine partner, Sheba

LIPTON, JAMES

The sycophantic host of cable's *Inside the Actors Studio* once attended a boxing match with Walken and intellectual gadabout George

Plimpton at Madison Square Garden. The evening ended in a bizarre confrontation with a group of African-American youths outside the arena. "The three of us looked at each other and thought, 'Well . . . what's this?'" Lipton later recalled. "And then the leader of them stepped forward, put his belly against Chris,' and said, 'Man, you are the coolest white man in America.' And, I said to Chris, 'That is the best compliment you will get as long as you live.'"

LOVE STORY

Walken tested for the part of Oliver Barrett IV in this 1970 romantic melodrama, which became an enormous worldwide hit and secured seven Oscar nominations. He wasn't alone. David Birney and Ken Howard also auditioned for the role, while Jon Voight, Michael Sarrazin, Michael Douglas, Michael York, Peter Fonda, Keith Carradine, Beau Bridges, and Jeff Bridges all turned it down. Walken was reportedly one of director Arthur Hiller's top choices for the part, but producer Robert Evans preferred Ryan O'Neal. All these years later, Walken doesn't sound too broken up about the missed opportunity. "I wouldn't have been any good," he told an interviewer in 2001.

LSD

Walken has admitted to taking LSD for the first time on November 9, 1965, during the New York City blackout. His companions for the evening were Vaughn Meader, the comedian best known for his impersonation of President John F. Kennedy, and actor Raul Julia. The three men were attending an acting class in Manhattan when the lights went out at around 5:30 pm. They headed out onto Seventh Avenue, where another classmate approached them and asked if they wanted to drop some acid. "So we went to where he lived and I took it," Walken says. "I must say I had a great time. I believe there was a full moon that night, what they call a bomber's moon, and the city was so beautiful."

See also **Drugs**.

LYMON, FRANKIE

This rock 'n' roll pioneer was a classmate of Walken's at the Professional Children's School in Manhattan. Lymon was only fourteen in 1956 when he and his group The Teenagers scored a huge international hit with "Why Do Fools Fall In Love?" He became a teen idol, then a **drug** addict. He died of a heroin overdose in 1968.

M TO N

MACY'S

As a teenager, Walken was rejected for a holiday job at the venerable New York City department store because he failed an adding and subtracting test.

MAN OF THE YEAR   ★★

Christopher Walken knows a little something about Internet-generated presidential fever (see **Walken for President**). In this 2006 feature, Robin Williams plays a late-night TV comic who becomes the beneficiary of a similar online campaign. In this case, he's propelled all the way to the White House—though vote-counting chicanery is to blame. Walken plays Jack Menken, Williams's craggy manager. He rolls through most of the movie in a wheelchair, chainsmoking cigarettes and barking out notes like an old time show business macher. Weirdly, *Man of the Year* was marketed as a wacky comedy in the style of Chris Rock's *Head of State*. It's not. It's a latter-day Frank Capra movie with a dark, conspiracy-themed undercurrent. Still, it's better than you might think—although critics panned it, and audiences avoided it like the plague.

MAN ON FIRE   ★★★

Walken must really enjoy working with Tony Scott. This is the second of three films he's made with the British-born director. It's almost as violent as *True Romance* and nearly as stylized as *Domino*. Denzel Washington stars as John Creasy, an ex-CIA man turned private bodyguard who goes on a bloody killing spree after a little girl gets kidnapped while under his protection. Walken plays Paul Rayburn, Creasy's old spy buddy—although he was originally tapped for the more villainous role that went to Mickey Rourke. The well-received 2004 release gave him a welcome opportunity to play against type. "Like the line in the film says, 'I'm finished with killing

PLAYING A JADED EX-CIA MAN, WALKEN HAS A NOSH
WITH DENZEL WASHINGTON IN *MAN ON FIRE*.

people,'" Walken says. "He's put that part of his life behind him, and so I played it very casual in that sense, and I hope I upset people's expectations in that way because I know I carry a certain amount of villainous baggage when it comes to these kinds of characters. This time, it felt much more interesting to be the good guy."

> *"Creasy's art is death. He's about to*
> *paint his masterpiece."*
> —Paul Rayburn, accurately forecasting his old CIA pal's impending rampage,
> in 2004's *Man on Fire*

MARCH 31

Walken's birthday, a date all Walkenphiles should have marked on their calendars.

MAX

In an oddity of casting, Walken has played a character named Max in three films to date: *A View to a Kill*, *Batman Returns*, and *Kiss Toledo Goodbye*.

> *"I like the name Max. If I had*
> *a kid, I'd name him Max."*
>
> —Walken, in a 2007 interview

MCBAIN   ★★★

The Deer Hunter meets *The Dogs of War* in this incredibly schlocky 1991 action feature, about a steely-eyed ex-POW who leads a group of fellow Vietnam vets on a mission to overthrow the corrupt president of Colombia. Walken stars as Bobby McBain, an implausibly urbane New York City construction worker whose taciturn façade hides the scars he bore in Indochina. He thought he'd put the memory of being tortured in a half-submerged bamboo cage behind him, until the sister of the man who saved him from the Vietcong shows up on his worksite one day with a heartbreaking tale of woe. Her brother's been killed by El Presidente, who's in cahoots with the Colombian **drug** cartel, and only McBain can help her liberate the country from narcoterrorists. (Why she thinks this is never explained.) Fortunately, McBain knows three or four guys who are willing to drop everything and travel to Colombia to settle the score. Assault Force McBain includes such obligatory action movie stock characters as a hotshot pilot, a McGyver-esque technical wizard, and a big, jovial black guy. A miscast Michael Ironside plays a moneybags pal of McBain's who bankrolls the operation. Come to think of it, everyone in *McBain* seems miscast, from Walken on down. The film feels like it was written for Chuck Norris or Jean-Claude Van Damme, with

Walken plugged in at the last minute. And it has a heavy-handed anti-drug message that is driven home with all the subtlety of the title character's jackhammer. "If you took the weight of all the people in Washington D.C. and turned it into gold," McBain explains at one point, "it would be less than the annual worldwide **drug** trade." Huh? He even agrees to take on the druglords in part to atone for getting stoned at Woodstock! One of the strangest choices Walken has made in his entire career, *McBain* nevertheless has a strange train wreck kind of appeal. Although it fizzled at the box office upon its initial release, the film has a hardcore cult following.

TRYING TO REMAKE HIMSELF AS AN ACTION HERO, WALKEN TOOK ON THE RAMBO-ESQUE TITLE ROLE IN 1991'S *MCBAIN*.

"You're going to be going to a lot of funerals—including your own."

—Bobby McBain, laying the smack down on a dapper Mafia don, in 1991's *McBain*

THE *MCBAIN* FILE

According to tallies posted on various websites, 240 people are shot to death, stabbed, or burned alive over the course of this movie.

- Director James Glickenhaus's other cinematic gems include *Frankenhooker and Maniac Cop.*

- The character of Bobby McBain bears more than a passing resemblance to Nick Chevotarevich, Walken's character in **The Deer Hunter.** Both men work with metal (Nick is a steel worker; McBain is an iron welder on a construction site.) Both men serve in Vietnam, where they are captured and brutalized in a bamboo cage. Both men are violently liberated and escape by helicopter.

- The film's Spanish title is *McBain: O Guerreiro Moderno (McBain: The Modern Warrior)*

- McBain sparked a mild controversy when the film's producers demanded that the animated TV series *The Simpsons* stop using the name "McBain" for its Arnold Schwarzenegger-inspired action hero character. Even though the *Simpsons'* McBain's existence predated the release of the film, Twentieth Century Fox agreed to refer to the cartoon character by his "real name," Rainier Wolfcastle, for several years to forestall any legal action.

MCKELLEN, IAN

Walken counts this distinguished English thespian among his "actor heroes." In 1967, Walken even wrote McKellen a letter to compliment him on his performance in a London stage production of Arbuzov's *The Promise*. It was the first fan letter Walken had ever written to a fellow actor.

I'LL PASS

He has a reputation for saying yes to any part that comes his way, but there have been rare instances when Walken has passed on a role. Here's a partial list of parts he's reported to have turned down—along with the name of the actor who eventually said yes.

FILM	ROLE	ACTOR
Exorcist II: The Heretic (1977)	Father Lamont	Richard Burton
Reservoir Dogs (1992)	Mr. Blonde	Michael Madsen
Judge Dredd (1995)	Rico	Armand Assante
From Dusk Till Dawn (1996)	Seth Gecko	George Clooney
Monkeybone (2001)	Death	Whoopi Goldberg

ME AND MY BROTHER   ★★

In 1968, Walken made his film debut in this experimental pseudo-documentary from director Robert Frank. *Me and My Brother* begins as a chronicle of the day-to-day activities of Julius Orlovsky, the catatonic brother of poet Peter Orlovsky, longtime companion of Allen Ginsberg. But the documentary quickly devolves into a film-within-a-film in which actors are hired to play the real people involved. Walken plays director Robert Frank, although all his dialogue is dubbed in the director's own voice—one of many strange, Brechtian touches in this weirdly compelling film. The *New York Times* called it "a disturbing but entirely graphic voyage into a still mysterious world."

MEASURE FOR MEASURE

Fresh off his success on Broadway in *The Lion in Winter*, Walken assumed the role of Claudio, the young nobleman sentenced to death for fathering a child out of wedlock, in the New York Shakespeare Festival production of *Measure for Measure* in Central Park in July 1966. At the time, Walken had no classical theater experience. ("I wore tights in [*Lion in Winter*], so they figured I could play Shakespeare," he later quipped.) To bone up for the part, he read **Shakespeare**'s speeches out loud to himself, without taking a breath, to make them sound more conversational.

The work paid off. In his *New York Times* review, Stanley Kauffmann compared the actor to Peter O'Toole, calling him "a natural actor, with a highly expressive face, immediate conviction, and quick sensitivity." "Mr. Walken should go a long way," Kauffmann concluded, "to the benefit of us all." Amen, brother.

MEET THE PARENTS

Reportedly, Walken turned down the part of Jack Byrnes, the eccentric former CIA operative in the 2000 comedy hit *Meet the*

Parents. The role went to Walken's *Deer Hunter* costar Robert De Niro instead.

MILAGRO BEANFIELD WAR, THE   ★★

Christopher Walken as a relentless federal agent in a cowboy hat? It sounds like the basis for a cinematic ten strike, but he's in far too little of director Robert Redford's twee fable about a water dispute in a tiny New Mexico town—and what little he is in isn't very interesting. A stoned-looking Walken sleepwalks through his role as Kyril

A BEAMING WALKEN INTERVENES IN A DISPUTE OVER IRRIGATION IN ROBERT REDFORD'S *THE MILAGRO BEANFIELD WAR*.

Montana, a laconic lawman who's dispatched by the government to apprehend a rebellious bean farmer accused of stealing water to irrigate his land. The film divided critics, many of whom found it insufferably precious and inconsistent in tone. Nevertheless, it gave Walken a chance to appear in a prestigious Hollywood production at a time when his career was in something of a rut. He also got to work with Redford, whom Walken found "very meticulous. He covered the scenes very well."

> ### "This posse couldn't find itself."
> —Kyril Montana, bemoaning the tracking skills of the local constabulary, in 1988's *The Milagro Beanfield War*

MIND SNATCHERS, THE ★★

"It's the day after tomorrow—and everything is under control," blared trailers for this moody 1972 feature, also known as *The Happiness Cage*. The stagy film—based on a play by Dennis Reardon—echoes themes that can be found in the superior *A Clockwork Orange* and *One Flew Over the Cuckoo's Nest*. In his first big-screen lead, Walken plays U.S. Army Private James Reese, an affectless loner who is apprehended after a violent outburst and incarcerated in a secluded mental hospital in the German countryside. There he is diagnosed as a schizophrenic and subjected to mind control experiments and brain surgery. Ronny Cox, best known for his turn as a doomed daytripper in *Deliverance*, delivers a "cuckoo for cocoa puffs" performance as Walken's antic cellmate, Sgt. Miles. Cox's capering is clearly intended to steal the show, but it only distracts from the drama and clashes with Walken's subdued, intense portrayal. The *New York Times* saw things the other way, however, praising Cox and decrying the "plastic shrewdness" of Walken's performance. DVD viewers can render their own judgment.

MILITARY DOCTORS PLAY WITH WALKEN'S HEAD IN THE
CAUTIONARY FEATURE *THE MIND SNATCHERS*.

One person who wasn't exactly delighted with *The Mind Snatchers* was
Walken himself. "That one was a piece of garbage," he told an interviewer in 1981. "And for a while, it seemed my career in film was
finished. I wasn't demoralized—I just felt that's the way it is, most
actors never even have a movie career."

MINEO, SAL

This future Oscar nominee attended the Professional Children's
School with Walken in the **1950s**. Praised for his kinetic perform-

ances opposite James Dean in *Rebel Without A Cause* and *Giant*, Mineo never capitalized on his early promise and drifted into show business obscurity. He was stabbed to death by a would-be mugger in 1976 at age thirty-seven.

MISTRESS   ★★

Walken has a blink-and-you'll-miss-him cameo in this 1992 comedy about a down-on-his-luck screenwriter's attempt to get his cherished film script produced in Hollywood. As a suicidal actor who jumps off a building in the middle of a scene, he has only a few lines of dialogue. Robert De Niro coproduced and costars. However, anyone hoping for a *Deer Hunter* reunion will be sorely disappointed. What little screen time Walken gets is shared instead with TV's *Arli$$*, Robert Wuhl.

MODELING

Walken began his career as a nude calendar model—at the age of fourteen months. "I posed naked snuggling with two **cats** for a series of calendar pictures, which were a big success," he later recalled. "I haven't seen those pictures in a long, long time, but I remember doing it—and I've always wondered what kind of cats those were. Finally, I've just accepted that they were just cats and I'll never know what kind."

> *"It sounds odd now, but when I was growing up, it wasn't. There were hundreds of kids who did that."*
>
> —Walken, on his career as a nude model

MOON WORSHIP

In a 1973 interview, Walken confessed that he spent "several years" worshipping the moon "as a sort of religious fanatic." "Moon cultures are maternalistic, and I'm a tremendous feminist," he explained, though he did not elaborate on precisely what rituals were involved. Eventually, he gave up the religion entirely. "I remained very close to the moon but I don't make myself miserable about her any more," he conceded.

> *"Moon cultures are much more ancient than sun cultures, and I think of myself as a sort of pre-Christian person."*
>
> —Walken, on his period of moon worship

"MORE COWBELL"
See Cowbell Sketch.

MOST PROMISING PERSONALITY OF 1966
Theater World conferred this distinction on Walken in 1967, acknowledging his work on stage in *The Rose Tattoo* the previous year.

MOUSEHUNT ★★
A wily mouse drives Walken off his ladder and into madness in this cartoonish 1997 feature. Nathan Lane and Lee Evans play moronic brothers who inherit a mansion inhabited by the world's most resourceful, impossible-to-kill rodent. They hire Walken, playing a manic exterminator, to help rid them of their unwanted houseguest. He drives around in a van with a giant mechanical cockroach on the roof and employs some of the same sniffing and tracking tics he used to hunt angels in *The Prophecy*. He also eats mouse feces. If that kind of humor turns you on, you'll enjoy this lightweight comedy. If not, at least stick around for Walken's twitching, frothing exit scene. It's the last amusing bit in the picture.

Although *Mousehunt* was aimed primarily at kids, Walken approached his role with the same gravity he brings to every part. To get in character as Caesar the exterminator, he walked around his property in Connecticut, which is home to more than a few field mice, trying to think like a rodent. In an interview to promote the film, Walken described a mouse's mindset as "a zen state . . . very peaceful, very, very aware. But I didn't get cheese cravings or anything like that."

> *"Although I usually play some sort of exterminator,*
> *it's not in a comedy."*

—Walken, rationalizing his participation in the 1997 comedy *Mousehunt*

"EXTERMINATE ALL THE BRUTES!" WALKEN PLAYS A PEST CONTROL MAN ON A MISSION IN *MOUSEHUNT*.

MUGGINGS

Walken has been mugged on at least two occasions. In October 1979, he was viciously beaten by two youths outside his Manhattan brownstone after he asked them to lower the volume on their boom box. (See **Ortiz Brothers Incident** for more details.) Eighteen years later, while filming *The Prophecy II* in Italy, he was accosted by two men posing as autograph seekers at the Venice airport. His script was stolen, along with his glasses, keys, driver's license, credit cards, and one hundred dollars in cash. A week later, Walken got a phone call from a Venetian acquaintance whose phone number he had written on the front page of the script. The friend informed him that a woman from Sicily had found his bag lying on the side of the road. "So I got the bag back with the script! All they took was the hundred bucks!" Walken crowed.

MUGGS, J. FRED

As a child actor working in New York's Rockefeller Center, Walken often encountered the bediapered, bicycling chimpanzee mascot of NBC's *Today Show*. "Mr. Muggs the chimpanzee," Walken fondly remembers. "He would drive up and down the hallways, and this was all I'd see every day."

MUSIC VIDEOS

Given his extraordinary dance skills, it's no surprise that Walken has appeared in a handful of music videos. The two most noteworthy examples are Madonna's "Bad Girl" (directed by Fight Club's David Fincher) and Fatboy Slim's "Weapon of Choice" (directed by Being John Malkovich's Spike Jonze), but Walken also pops up in Duran Duran's "A View to a Kill" (via clips from the 1985 James Bond film).

MUSICALS

Walken cut his show business teeth in stage musicals, working as a chorus boy on Broadway in shows like *High Spirits* and *Baker Street* and travelling the country in a touring production of *West Side Story*. On screen, he's made memorable appearances in the movie musicals *Pennies from Heaven* and *Hairspray*. In an earlier era, he believes he could have been the next Gordon MacRae. "I think that if I had grown up and had been in show business and the movies fifteen, thirty years earlier, I think I would have made a lot more musical movies," Walken says. "I could have made a dent there."

MYSTERY OF NATALIE WOOD, THE

Walken is depicted as a clueless dolt in this cheesy 2004 made-for-TV biopic about the doomed screen idol, who costarred with him in 1982's *Brainstorm*. Australian actor Malcolm Kennard, who could not look less like the man he is portraying, wisely declines to mimic Walken's distinctive vocal style. At times he sounds more like Rick Moranis doing his Woody Allen impression. The Walken character appears only in the film's final act, set in and around the boat where Wood accidentally drowned in 1981. Directed by Peter Bogdanovich, *The Mystery of Natalie Wood* was authorized and co-produced by **Wood**'s younger sister, Lana. It largely steers clear of controversy, offering no new dubious claims about her cause of death.

NAKED CITY   ★★★

Billed under his real name of **Ronnie** Walken, Walken made a January 1963 appearance on this prime-time police procedural, the *Law and Order* of its day. In an episode awkwardly entitled "Robin Hood and Clarence Darrow, They Went Out with Bow and Arrow," Walken plays Chris Johannis, the disaffected teenage son of a depressed, widowed liquor store proprietor played by Eddie Albert. When Albert's best friend is shot and killed in a holdup, he decides to take the law into his own hands in an effort to prove himself a hero to his sons. The fact that they're likely to wind up as orphans in the bargain doesn't seem to occur to him. It's not one of the better *Naked City* episodes, and Walken's performance is somewhat stilted, but it's worth watching just to see him denounce the world of stuck-up squares in dialogue that sounds like it should be accompanied by bongo taps in a jazz café.

NECKTIES

Walken hates them and refuses to wear one, even under a sport coat or suit jacket. "I don't like neckties, or any kind of strangulating object," he says. As a youth, Walken received necktying instruction from child star **Brandon De Wilde**.

NEW ROSE HOTEL   ★★★

Walken's fourth collaboration with director **Abel Ferrara** is a stylish neo-noir adaptation of a short story by science fiction writer William Gibson. Set in the near future, *New Rose Hotel* follows corporate pirates X (Willem Dafoe) and Fox (Walken) as they hatch a plan to entice a brilliant geneticist to defect from one global multinational to another. Wearing a white suit and twirling his cane like a cyberpunk Willie Wonka, Walken is given free rein to overact, while Dafoe plays straight man. A scene set in a restaurant, in which Walken drops his improvised calling card "**Cole slaw for everybody**," is especially amusing. Also amused was actress Asia Argento, who got to work with two of the most volatile actors in the business. "I don't usually care for actors because they're seldom creative, but those two were great," she said. "Walken's performance was brilliant. He was so completely out of his mind, so incredibly angry, that he couldn't remember his lines. We always had to keep big sheets of paper tacked up with his words written on them."

"Also-rans make me puke."

—Fox (Walken), explaining his business philosophy to X (Willem Dafoe) in 1998's *New Rose Hotel*

WALKEN'S PORTRAYAL OF A SUAVE LADIES' MAN IN *NEXT STOP GREENWICH VILLAGE* WAS ONE OF THE HIGH POINTS OF HIS EARLY "GIGOLO" PERIOD.

NEXT STOP, GREENWICH VILLAGE   ★★

In the defining performance of his early "gigolo" period, Walken plays a jaded playwright who preys on other guy's girlfriends in this semi-autobiographical 1976 film from director Paul Mazursky. Lenny Baker plays a nebbish from Brooklyn who pursues a career in show business. Walken—billed as Chris Walken in the opening credits and **Christopher** Walken in the end credits—plays Robert, an oleaginous goyishe playa who sleeps with everything that moves. The two men clash. Walken wins. Baker moves on. Walken's performance consists mainly of staring into space with a disaffected smirk on his face. He won the role after Mazursky saw him in his Obie Award-winning performance as *Kid Champion* off-Broadway.

NICK OF TIME   ★★★

In *The Dead Zone*, Walken played a good man compelled to commit a seemingly unjustifiable act of political assassination for noble reasons he can't disclose. In *Nick of Time*, the shoe's on the other foot. This time Walken plays a slimy villain who tries to blackmail the virtuous Johnny Depp into assassinating the governor of California. The noble cause? Saving the life of Depp's young daughter, whom Walken will have killed if Depp doesn't follow through in the allotted time period. *Nick of Time* has all the makings of a classic thriller. It unfolds in real time, which gives it a clockwork urgency reminiscent of *High Noon* or TV's *24*. Walken delivers one of his most unsavory portrayals as Mr. Smith, a homicidal gubernatorial security man who seems to have attended the *Night of the Hunter* School of Day Care. He makes what could have been idle threats against a helpless child sound all too believable. Devious, snarling, and seemingly all-seeing, he's also more than a match for Johnny Depp's hapless hero, whom he repeatedly brutalizes with spontaneous kneecappings and kicks to the groin. Walken is so good, in fact, he almost makes you forget about the shaky premise and numerous implausible plot twists. Charles S. Dutton and Marsha Mason also star.

Behind the scenes, *Nick of Time* was a labor of love for Walken. He got to work with Johnny Depp for the first time. (The two would team up again four years later in Tim Burton's *Sleepy Hollow*.) Best of all, virtually the entire film took place inside Los Angeles's Bonaventure Hotel, making it a breeze to shoot. "You'd go to your room for lunch, go back downstairs and get to work," Walken explained. "That's the way to do it." Perhaps some enterprising producer will take the hint and offer Walken a starring role in a revival of the popular nighttime soap *Hotel*.

"*I'll make gravy out of your little girl!*"
—Walken, doing his best Big Bad Wolf imitation, as the murderous Mr. Smith
in 1995's *Nick of Time*

NIGHT OF 100 STARS 2

Walken cut a rug as part of an all-star tap line on this March 1985 TV variety special. It was producer Alexander Cohen's second of three *Night of 100 Stars* extravaganzas, in which **dancing** celebrities were trotted out and sequentially numbered with an on-screen graphic. For the record, Walken is star number 99, right between actress Nanette Fabray and ballerina Cynthia Gregory. Still sporting the outlandish blonde dye job he donned for the **James Bond** film *A View to a Kill*, Walken appears in the garish showstopping tap number "A Pair of Shoes." He gets to hoof it alongside such Broadway and Hollywood legends as Chita Rivera, Donald O'Connor, Dick Van Dyke, and Ginger Rogers—not to mention Donny Osmond! Tapping TV stars Georgia Engel (*The Mary Tyler Moore Show*), Beth Howland (*Alice*), and Bonnie Franklin (*One Day at a Time*) are also on hand. Of all the assembled performers, Walken seems to be having the most fun.

1950s

Walken appears to have mixed feelings about the decade in which he came of age. He credits it for helping to shape his personality. "My main influence would have been the fifties," he has said. "The *American Graffiti* atmosphere, which was in a strange way very sanitized, extremely odd, but great." Elsewhere, Walken has described the decade as "one of the most stupid times" in United States history. "The fifties," he once told an interviewer, "were one of the dumbest things that ever happened to America."

NOSTRADAMUS

Walken has identified this sixteenth century French apothecary and seer as the historical figure he'd most like to portray. He did come close once—playing an eighteenth century French alchemist and clairvoyant in 2001's *The Affair of the Necklace*.

O TO P

OKLAHOMA!

This classic Rodgers and Hammerstein musical opened on Broadway the night Walken was born—**March 31**, 1943.

OPIUM

Walken indulged in a little "Chinese molasses" while filming *The Deer Hunter* in Thailand in 1977. "Somebody gave me some and I didn't know what to do with it, so I ate it," he later recalled. The experience made him sick to his stomach, so Walken consulted a physician upon his return to the United States. The doctor concluded that Walken's midnight oil had been cut with water buffalo dung—hence the intestinal bug. "It lasted a long time," the actor remembers—long enough to put him off "God's medicine" for good.

    See also **Drugs.**

OPPORTUNISTS, THE   ★★

A reformed safecracker finds that life on the straight and narrow isn't all it's cracked up to be in this 2000 indie feature. Walken plays against type as Vic Kelly, a sad sack auto mechanic trying desperately to live down his criminal past. His doting girlfriend (Cyndi Lauper) keeps offering him loans to help him scale a crushing mountain of debts, but the lure of one last big score proves too much. Vic signs on for what looks like an easy heist, with predictably dicey consequences. Indie vets Vera Farmiga and Donal Logue also star.

    As usual, Walken tapped an everyman vein for his quietly effective portrayal of this conflicted ex-con. "He's a guy who's like us all," he said of Vic Kelly. "He needs a little bit of a break. He'd done some dumb things and paid. He's just looking to get out from under which I think a lot of people can identify with. He's a guy with good intentions who's made mistakes. He did some stupid things and basically he's just trying to have a nice life."

Although it won't make anyone forget *King of New York*, *The Opportunists* is an agreeably grungy caper film with some authentic outer borough New York atmosphere—hardly surprising, since it was filmed on location in Queens, just a few blocks from where Walken was born. "That's my neighborhood where they shot the movie. The house that I live in in the movie is about two miles from where my parents live now." In fact, during filming, Walken would routinely pass by the apartment building he lived in when he was a baby in **Astoria**, NY. "The curious thing is that the neighborhood hasn't changed that much in all those years."

"The regular citizen thing is not going too good."

—Vic Kelly, pining for his days as safecracker in 2000's *The Opportunists*

ORTIZ BROTHERS INCIDENT

"Growing up in New York is like living in a horror museum," Walken once observed, "because there are so many strange people walking the streets and riding the subways. You learn to develop a tough front if you live here, just in case you get into any kind of trouble and you need to talk your way out of it." Perhaps he was reflecting on his own violent encounter with two such unsavory New York characters, William and Samuel Ortiz, in October 1979.

According to published reports confirmed by Walken in subsequent interviews, the incident took place outside Walken's brownstone on Manhattan's Upper West Side. The boisterous Ortiz siblings were cranking their boom box to the max as Walken left his home to visit the corner store. "I said to one of them 'Turn down the music,'" Walken says, and "I don't think I was nice about it. The other guy started swinging at me. I was protecting myself from him when the first guy got a stick from the garbage can and broke my nose with it.

He could have knocked my eye out." Walken's finger was also broken in the assault. He later developed an infection and had to undergo surgery, forcing him to drop out of the Yale Repertory Theater's production of *Measure for Measure* that December.

In February 1980, the Ortiz Brothers pled guilty to assaulting Walken, although they insisted they wouldn't have done anything if Walken had just asked them politely to turn down the volume. Walken disputed that claim. "I figure if I'm being violated, amenities are beside the point," he declared. The Ortizes got off with brief prison sentences, a development that left Walken angry and embittered toward the justice system. "It's a good thing I'm an actor and have some money," he fumed. "I'd hate to think what would happen to some poor nine-to-five guy, somebody without the luxury of time and money. I tell you, I really got banged around. It's probably just New York City—I mean, I love New York, but the tedious machinations of the legal system are depressing. You can rob someone's house, cut him up, smash him with a brick, and the law won't pay any attention to you. You have to murder someone in cold blood before they'll take you seriously." Elsewhere, he acidly concluded: "I decided to go to court, and I went in with a tremendous respect for the law and walked out with a healthy disrespect."

> *"People who know me weren't surprised it happened. I live in New York City and I'm a wise guy. All I did was go up to those two guys and tell them to turn down their radio."*
>
> —Walken, on his bout of "boom box rage" in October 1979

OSBOURNE, OZZY

In 2006, erroneous reports on the Internet had Walken taking on the role of the bathead-biting Satanic rocker in a movie based on Mötley

Crüe's band biography *The Dirt*. Crüe member Nikki Sixx actually blamed Walken for starting the false rumor. "I think he had a couple drinks and it got blown out of proportion," said Sixx, whose real name is Frank Ferrana.

OSCAR

Walken took home the Academy Award for Best Supporting Actor for *The Deer Hunter*, in a ceremony held on April 9, 1979, at the Dorothy Chandler Pavilion in Los Angeles. The other nominees in

FLANKED BY PRESENTERS TELLY SAVALAS AND DYAN CANNON, WALKEN EXULTS IN HIS OSCAR WIN FOR *THE DEER HUNTER*.

Walken's category that year were Bruce Dern for *Coming Home*, Richard Farnsworth for *Comes a Horseman*, Jack Warden for *Heaven Can Wait*, and John Hurt for *Midnight Express*. Presenting Walken his award were Dyan Cannon and his one-time *Kojak* costar, Telly Savalas. Dressed in a tuxedo and sporting a weird walrus moustache, the happy winner arrived on stage to the tune of Frankie Valli's "Can't Take My Eyes Off of You" and delivered a perfunctory thirty-six-word acceptance speech.

After the ceremony, Walken and his wife **Georgianne** attended a small private party with Meryl Streep and her family, then retired to their hotel room. Walken describes the scene: "The management had sent up a bottle of champagne, my agent was in the room with a couple of people, I was holding the Oscar. Then everybody left and we went to bed and I said to my wife, with the Oscar in my hand, 'This is a house.' And it was. I was holding our house in my hand. I knew that's what it meant." Some reports have Walken going to bed with the statuette in his arms that night.

These days, Walken keeps his Oscar in a blue slipcover in an alcove in his house in Connecticut. "I keep it in a quiet, respectful place. I keep its cover on, for the same reason my mother used to keep covers on everything, so it doesn't fade."

SHORT AND SWEET

Here is Walken's Academy Award acceptance speech, in its entirety:

Thank you, Michael. I'm very happy to have this. I salute Michael Cimino with this Oscar here tonight and I'd like to add my thanks to the members of the Academy and to Mr. Robert De Niro. Thank you all.

OTHELLO

With his hair dyed maroon, sporting a **black** leather jacket he once wore in a production of *Oklahoma!*, Walken put a punk twist on the role of Iago in a 1991 New York Shakespeare Festival production of **Shakespeare**'s classic tragedy. Walken's old **LSD** buddy Raul Julia played the jealous Moor. Critics were bitterly divided by the unconventional production. "Christopher Walken makes Iago his own, alternating between obsequious camaraderie and the contemporary street-smart cynicism of someone who feels perpetually short-changed," raved *Theater Week*. The *New York Times* was decidedly less impressed. "Walken looks to have stepped out of a sleazy motorcycle film set in the indeterminate future when law and order (and diction) have disappeared from the planet," its reviewer sneered. "Even Iago's wit is reduced to something uncomfortably close in rhythm and emphasis to Jackie Mason shtick."

PAINTING

When he's not **cooking**, Walken can often be found painting—usually on his driveway. Because he can't draw, he prefers abstracts—or "big schmear paintings," as he calls them. "I don't mix colors up too much," he told London's *Daily Telegraph* in 2002. "I like clear reds and yellows and greens and orange. My paintings are not a mess. They are sort of neat abstracts. Very colorful, but not about anything in particular; they are not bowls of fruit or anything. But very nice, very pleasant." He tends to work in frenzied spurts. He can go for long months without touching a brush to canvas, and then suddenly get the bug. "I'll go crazy for two weeks—go crazy just painting, painting, painting."

For years, Walken pursued his passion in secret, sharing his paintings only with close friends. "I just can't seem to get up the nerve to go and ask someone to put them in a gallery," he said. "I know some actors who do that and my paintings are better than theirs." With the advent of online auctioneering, he considered marketing his work through the Internet. "I was thinking about eBay, because I like to paint, and it occurred to me: 'What would happen if I put a painting on eBay? You think I could sell it?'" Eventually he overcame his trepidation and did convince a gallery to exhibit his work. The DCA Gallery in New York City hosted Walken's debut exhibition in the spring of 2003. "They sold most of the paintings," Walken reported afterwards. "They were cheap."

PAPP, JOE

This legendary New York stage impresario was one of Walken's early show business mentors. In the late 1960s, "I used to feed lines to actors for him," Walken once related. "I got very close to him. He used to call me 'my friend, the actor.'" That relationship started to pay off in 1974, when Walken's theatrical career was at a standstill. Reduced to playing Harry Houdini in a summer stock production of the magician's life in the Berkshires, Walken pleaded with Papp for help. "I went to [Joe] and I said, 'Nothing's going on, I'm collecting unemployment,'" Walken told *Shout* magazine in 2001. "And he said, 'Don't worry, I'm gonna put you in three plays in a row.' And he did. He was an amazing guy." The three plays, for the record, were *Troilus and Cressida*, *The Tempest*, and *Macbeth*—meaty **Shakespeare** parts that helped rehabilitate Walken's reputation as a classical actor. His summer stock days were over.

After that intervention, Papp occasionally summoned Walken back to the boards with offers of plum stage parts. "He'd call me on the phone and say, 'Do you want to play **Coriolanus**?' I'd say, 'Sure.' And he'd say, 'Well, why don't you read it first?' I'd say, 'Okay, but I'll do it anyway.'" The two remained close until Papp's death in October 1991. "The last time I saw him I was doing *Othello* in Central Park," Walken recalls. "He had been very ill. His son had died. It was all very sad. Iago opens the show, and the thing about Central Park is that they always start about twenty minutes before it gets dark. So if you're in the first scene, it's very intimidating, especially with Iago talking to the audience. So you look out there and you see your mother and your family and the critics and the actors who didn't get the job. You see everybody. And then I saw Joe. He was just sitting there. And then it got dark and I never saw him again."

PENNIES FROM HEAVEN   ★★★

Walken shakes what his momma gave him in a high-energy dance number in this 1981 **musical** from director Herbert Ross. Walken has called *Pennies from Heaven*, which gave him his first opportunity to dance on film, "a turning point in my life."

Based on a popular BBC television drama of the late 1970s,

PENNIES FROM HEAVEN GAVE WALKEN AN EARLY CHANCE TO DANCE ON SCREEN—AND HE MADE THE MOST OF IT.

"RACK 'EM UP." WALKEN SHOOTS SOME STICK
AS A PIMP IN *PENNIES FROM HEAVEN*.

Pennies from Heaven stars Steve Martin as a Depression-era sheet music salesman wrongly implicated in the murder of a young blind woman. Walken plays Tom, a tap-dancing pimp who lures Martin's mistress (Bernadette Peters) into a life of prostitution. He was originally offered a different part—that of the sad sack accordion player played by Vernal Bagneris—but opted to turn it down. Enter **Danny Daniels**, Walken's **childhood** tap instructor, who was choreographing the film. "I told Herbert to offer the part of the pimp to Chris," Daniels recalled. "Herb said, 'But he has to dance.' And when I told him how good a dancer he was Herb was delighted and the next thing I knew we were working together again."

Walken's show-stopping number, which combines elements of tap, striptease, and some athletic leaping, was completed in about five takes. Each time, Walken performed the entire number straight through without a stop. His jump onto a speakeasy bar, completed with the aid of an unseen mini-trampoline, is especially impressive. For a while, however, it didn't look like the sequence was going to come off at all. "My **dance** number was lying there like a pancake," he told interviewers in 1986. "I said 'How are you going to do this when nobody's looking? This is a performance for an audience.'" Walken then proceeded to enlist the aid of the production crew to serve as his personal peanut gallery, encouraging them to cheer on his performance. "The whole number just took off," he recalled. From that moment on, Walken has routinely asked technicians on his movie sets to look at him while he performs his scenes.

Although *Pennies from Heaven* garnered mixed reviews and bombed at the box office, the film's reputation has grown in recent years. It remains a bit of a revelation for those who have never seen Walken dance on camera—at least until 2000's "**Weapon of Choice**." "It was as if you found out De Niro was a chorus dancer," Meryl Streep once remarked. "But *Pennies From Heaven*—that's closer to the real guy." Walken himself holds a special place in his heart for the film. "I'm very happy to have done that because it was the last **musical** ever made by MGM," he says. "I remember that I dubbed my taps on the same little parquet floor that Fred Astaire, Gene Kelly and Donald O'Connor, all those people, used."

One person who remained immune to *Pennies from Heaven*'s charms was **Fred Astaire** himself. Although he complimented Walken on his dancing at a party after the premiere, he offered a bilious review of the film as a whole: "I have never spent two more miserable hours in my life. Every scene was cheap and vulgar. They didn't realize that the thirties were a very innocent age, and that it should have been set in the eighties—it was just froth; it makes you cry it's so distasteful."

PHILBIN, REGIS

During a 2004 appearance on *Live with Regis and Kelly*, Walken expressed his desire to costar in a film with the genial **television** gabber. To Philbin's delight, he proceeded to outline a possible scenario—"a buddy movie caper type of thing on motorcycles"— that, sadly, remains unrealized to date.

PIRATES OF THE CARIBBEAN: THE CURSE OF THE BLACK PEARL

Walken was considered for the role of Captain Jack Sparrow in this 2003 megahit based on the popular Disney theme park ride. Bill Murray, Robin Williams, and Steve Martin were also in the running for the part, which went to Johnny Depp.

POCONOS

As a child, Walken had a soul-deadening experience attending summer camp in the Pennsylvania mountain range. He later drew upon that experience to form his Oscar-winning portrayal of a tormented

Vietnam vet in *The Deer Hunter.* "I remember very clearly in the scenes when I lost my marbles that I remembered as a kid the couple times I went to summer camp. It was just awful. It was in the Poconos. I remember being so miserable. I was really in despair. To me, the end of that movie is just like camp."

POKER

"I'm a terrible poker player," Walken concedes. "I can't hide my hand. Everybody knows what I've got." Nevertheless, he enjoys watching professional poker tournaments on **television** and is astonished at the large amounts bet on every hand. "If I played, I would never place five dollars unless I had a royal flush. If somebody saw me bet, they'd say, 'Oh, forget it,' because I'd have, like, four aces or something."

POLICE

Although he's occasionally played lawmen on film (see *All-American Murder* and *The Milagro Beanfield War*), Walken usually finds himself on the other side of the cop/criminal divide. Perhaps his admitted phobia about the police has something to do with it. "I'm very scared of cops and the law," he has said. "That was part of growing up in the fifties, when authority, badges, and uniforms were very intimidating."

PONZI SCHEME

In the 1980s, Walken was the victim of a fraudulent investment operation run by his mother-in-law's boss. He lost hundreds of thousands of dollars in the scam, which involved sending money to a dubious investment manager in Chicago who promised an implausibly high rate of return. "It was my fault for not paying attention," Walken admits. "My wife, thinking she was doing me a favor, got me involved in it. . . . At the time it was all the money I had. I was a real jerk."

POOLHALL JUNKIES   ★★

Walken chalks up his cue as a mysterious millionaire who bankrolls a pool-playing prodigy in writer/director/star Mars Callahan's 2003 indie drama. He plays "Uncle Mike," an eccentric moneybags who knows his way around a billiard table and just happens to carry oodles of cash in a metal attaché case. When Callahan's reformed pool hustler runs afoul of another shark, played by Chazz Palminteri, Walken is there in a flash to back him up and stiffen his spine with a weird monologue about lions eating hyenas in the jungle.

Not surprisingly, Callahan wrote the part with Walken in mind. It then took him ten years to get the film made. Securing Walken's participation would be a major selling point. "I was in a play in New York and Mars came to see it," Walken says. "And he told me this film he was doing. He sent me the script." Walken was the first actor to sign on to the project—an important coup for the first-time director. "He didn't get on the phone and make phone calls and say, 'Hey, do this movie,'" said Callahan, "but he might as well have, because every actor in this business wants to work with Christopher Walken. He's one of the most appealing actors to work with. It became substantially easier to cast the film after Christopher Walken." In addition to Palminteri, the cast also includes Ricky Schroder as a hotshot hustler and Rod Steiger—in his final performance—as a kindly pool hall proprietor.

Walken's scenes took just over a week to shoot. Actor Michael Rosenbaum, who plays Callahan's brother in the film, vividly recalls the first day on the set. "The first day of shooting I walk up to Christopher Walken and Mars is standing there and I said, 'Should I call you Mr. Walken or should I call you Chris?' He looks at me and goes, 'Call me Flash.' Don't ask me why. . . . The next conversation I look up and I say, 'You know what? We all have the same **hair**. It's good hair. We have nice hair.' He goes, "I think that should be one of

WALKEN PONDERS THE GREEN FELT AS AN ENIGMATIC
MONEY MAN IN *POOLHALL JUNKIES*.

my first lines in the movie. I think I'm gonna say 'Nice hair.'" And he did."

"Don't beat him. Kick his ass."

—Uncle Mike, giving his protégé a pre-game pep talk for his grudge match against
Ricky Schroder, in 2003's *Poolhall Junkies*

POPCORN SHRIMP   ★

In 2001, Walken made his directorial debut with this five-minute short film starring Karate Kid Ralph Macchio and rapper Master P. "The same people who did the cooking show [*Cooking with Chris*] came to me," Walken says. "They were doing five-minute shorts. They had a bunch of actors do their own pieces and they asked me. I hung up the phone and wrote it." Filming on *Popcorn Shrimp*—about a case of mistaken identity involving a group of dodgy looking diners— took all of seven hours to complete. "It was done so quickly that I just said, 'Do whatever you want,'" Walken bragged. "I enjoy it when directors say that to me."

The hastiness showed. "It was awful," Walken declared of the finished product. At an August 2001 reception for his online fan club, Walken called the film "indecipherable and incomprehensible." Elsewhere he admitted that the *Popcorn Shrimp* experience "demonstrated that I'd be a lousy director."

"I wasn't good."

—Walken, on his work as writer/director of the inscrutable short film *Popcorn Shrimp*

PORNOGRAPHY

"I think it's very important for everybody to be able to look at anything," Walken once told an interviewer. In the late 1960s, this included adult films, which Walken's friends showed at home using the side of an icebox as a makeshift screen. "You get a very fine picture on the side of an icebox—extremely clear," he admitted. The grungy sixteen-millimeter stag loops (in which participants often kept their shoes and socks on during sex scenes) had a tendency to crack and burn in the projector, requiring Walken and his buds to stitch them back together with Scotch tape.

Walken nearly took the next step toward a career as an adult film distributor during a trip to Copenhagen in the early 1970s. He attended a live sex show during which a porno version of *Snow White and the Seven Dwarves* was shown. "All the dwarfs were doing her, then the devil came at the end and the wicked witch and it became an orgy—all very well done," Walken recalls. "I could have bought it for seventy-five dollars but somebody said to me, 'Don't take a chance, you'll get into trouble coming into America.'" Scared off by the prospect of being busted at the airport with the *Snow White* reel in his luggage, Walken passed on the chance to become an international porno purveyor.

> *"Pornos are like looking through a keyhole, and it seems to me maybe that's what all movies are all about."*
>
> —Walken, on his appreciation of pornography

PRACTICAL JOKES

Walken is fond of playing tricks on his costars. One of his favorite ruses involves pretending that it is his birthday and everyone's forgotten about him. "You can only do it once a movie," he says. "I get up early and I'm in the makeup chair at six in the morning. I pretend that I'm sad. Sooner or later, someone says, 'Chris, what's wrong? You look a little sad.' And I say, 'Well, it's my birthday and

I'm all alone . . .' But the key thing is to say after that, 'make sure you don't tell anyone.' Then around lunchtime, they have a cake, maybe some gifts or champagne."

Another of Walken's favorite gags plays off his reputation as a **moon-worshipping** weirdo. "Sometimes when they call for me to be on set, I'll stand outside my trailer and look up at the sky for a long time. A really long time. Finally, someone will ask, 'What are you looking at?' Next thing you know, you have ten people standing looking up at the sky for no particular reason. Then I'll just casually walk off."

Walken also indulged in some fecal japery while filming *Around the Bend* in New Mexico in 2003. Inspired by the ubiquity of cow dung mounds in the desert, he started giving them out to unsuspecting members of the crew. "You can pick up a [sun-dried] cowpie," Walken explained, "and you can walk up to somebody and say, 'Would you hold this please?' And they'll always take it!"

> ### *"What can I say? I just love cake."*
>
> —Walken, to actor Seann William Scott, after pulling his patented "birthday gag" on him on the set of 2003's *The Rundown*

PRESLEY, ELVIS

The dearly departed King of Rock 'n' Roll is one of Walken's show business heroes. He first became infatuated at age fifteen, when a girl he wanted to take to the prom showed him a magazine photo of her "boyfriend"—Elvis Presley. "This guy looked like a Greek god," Walken said. "Then I saw him on **television**. I loved everything about him."

Soon after he first saw Elvis, Walken changed his **hair**style to emulate him—and hasn't changed it since. "Maybe it's a little shorter, or a little longer, but the suggestion of Elvis is always there," he says. Often, when he's performing a scene with another actor, Walken will secretly pretend that he's Elvis. "I'm doing Elvis and this guy doesn't know I'm doing Elvis. I do it when things are getting stale. I'll do it to, like, juice things up a little." Walken is so enamored of the King that he devoted his first play, *Him*, to an exploration of Elvis' **afterlife** in limbo.

PROFESSIONAL CHILDREN'S SCHOOL

Walken received his earliest professional training at this prestigious show business academy on Manhattan's Upper West Side. It provided a chance to **dance** and act, along with a schedule flexible enough to allow him to audition. But the best part of all was the gender profile of the student body. "It was like 95 percent girls—beautiful girls," Walken later recalled. "They were all models and stuff. And the other boys were usually strange—what you might call 'scientific types.' They played the violin and the cello." Calling it "the most incredible setup a guy could ever want," Walken recalls that he never had any trouble getting a date. "I don't think I ever seriously spoke to another man until I was twenty-two."

> *"It was like that movie where the guy gets stranded on a planet of women."*
>
> —Walken, on his years at the Professional Children's School

PROPHECY, THE

There's a war in heaven—and everyone's invited! That's the basic premise of this grisly Bible-themed horror movie, which became an unlikely cult hit in 1995 and spawned a series of increasingly inferior sequels. Elias Koteas and Virginia Madsen are the nominal leads of *The Prophecy*, but they are (almost literally) blown off the screen by Walken in one of his most superfueled performances as the Archangel Gabriel, a misanthropic former capo in "God's Army" presently waging war on Heaven. He wants to return things to the way they were before Earth's "talking monkeys" displaced angels on the Lord's Christmas card list. For reasons that are never clearly explained, the key to his battle plan involves capturing the evil soul of a U.S. Army general who committed unspeakable atrocities during the Korean War. When the soul winds up in the body of an adorable little Native American girl, the chase is on!

The tone of *The Prophecy* is wildly uneven. Some actors play it straight, while others go the tongue-in-cheek route. As a good angel who meets a fiery end, Eric Stoltz does a beatific variation on his *Pulp Fiction* weirdo. Steve Hytner (best known for playing Kenny Bania on *Seinfeld*) has a cameo as a mordant medical examiner, while Adam Goldberg and Amanda Plummer vie for the Dwight Frye Award as a couple of would-be suicides whom Gabriel brings back from the brink of eternal sleep and forces into zombified servitude. In the end, of course, the film belongs to Walken. Liberally slathered in white pancake makeup and once again sporting the outlandish **black** bob he wore throughout 1995, he looks for all the world "like the corpse of Prince Valiant," in the words of the *San Francisco Chronicle*. He spits out his lines with savage glee and looks disquietingly at home in scenes where he's required to sniff a trail of blood on a piece of furniture or French kiss a man's unburied body. "I'm a lot of fun in that movie," Walken has said. "I enjoyed playing this angel who's furious at human beings and just kicks the shit out of everybody." In this case, "kicking the shit" generally entails ripping out the still-beating hearts of his angelic nemeses from their chest cavities, while spewing lines like: "I kill firstborns while their mamas watch. I turn cities into salt. I even, when I feel like it, rip the souls from little girls—and from now till kingdom come, the only thing you can count on in your existence is never understanding why."

There are a lot of things that defy understanding in *The Prophecy*. Like why Gabriel, who can kill with the touch of his hand, doesn't

THE ARCHANGEL GABRIEL MEETS HIS GORY END
—OR SO WE THOUGHT—IN *THE PROPHECY*.

simply incinerate the humans who get in his way on first sight, instead of letting them live on to foil his plans for celestial domination. Or why he's impervious to bullets in some scenes and not others. Or why an angel needs a zombie chauffeur to get him around town in the first place. Still, if you put aside those logical concerns, this is an entertaining religious shocker on par with *The Omen* and Walken's own *The Sentinel*. In the end, Gabriel is beaten to submission with a tire iron and has his heart ripped out and eaten by an enraged Lucifer (Viggo Mortensen). You might think that would kill him—but no,

Gabe and his magic trumpet return for another round of eschatological mayhem in 1998's *The Prophecy II*.

"Have a mint—on me."

—The Archangel Gabriel, capering with a group of schoolchildren in 1995's *The Prophecy*.

CHILD'S PLAY

By all accounts, Walken was at his most playful on the set of **The Prophecy**. Director Gregory Widen gave him *carte blanche* to improvise and experiment with different line readings. Nowhere is that more evident than in an early scene where Gabriel cavorts with a group of schoolchildren while surreptitiously examining their mouths for the presence of the dark soul he's been searching for. It's a chilling sequence that evokes memories of the classic Universal horror films of the 1930s and 40s. Said Walken: "It's a marvelous scene. They shot it very fast. Everything's very spontaneous with kids. But what I did was, when we went to shoot it, I walked up, and I'm all in black and I'm coming up like Frankenstein, and I said to the director: 'Don't tell them I'm playing a villain—just tell them it's Chris.' So he took me over to meet them and they're, like, playing among themselves, and he said, 'This is Chris,' and we all started to joke, and they didn't know I was a bad guy. If they'd been told by their mother or something, "Oh, here comes the boogie man," it would have been totally different. They didn't know anything. They treated me like I was . . . their daddy. It's very interesting."

PROPHECY II, THE   ★★★

Walken returns for more sniffing and killing as the malevolent Archangel Gabriel in this 1998 follow-up to 1995's *The Prophecy*.

This time, the plot is even more incoherent and the supporting cast even lower down on the Hollywood **food** chain. In fact, of the original cast, only Walken and Steve "Kenny Bania" Hytner return for this installment. (You know a film must be pretty bad when even Virginia Madsen passes on it.)

Still, Walken soldiers on, as does a game, if less than stellar cast led by Flashdancer Jennifer Beals as a lonely nurse who finds herself knocked up after a one-night stand with a hunky angel named Danyael (Russell Wong). Apparently, she's now carrying the savior of humanity—although it's never made clear why, or what purpose Gabriel has in mind for chasing after her. (Question: if Gabriel is really the leader of a vast angel "army," why is he always alone in his missions on Earth? Shouldn't he be bringing a crew with him?) Released from "the basement" (i.e., Hell) to which he was consigned at the end of the previous picture (well, actually he was killed, but we're encouraged to forget that minor detail), Gabriel is even madder, badder, and more dangerous to know in this chapter of the saga. Fittingly, Walken is even more over-the-top in his portrayal. With his blue mascara, **black** leather pants, and ghostly pallor, he looks like Christopher Lee's *Dracula* crossed with Data the android from *Star Trek: The Next Generation*. As usual, inconsistencies abound. Gabriel is fluent in colloquial expressions like "dirt nap," but has no idea what a radio is. Once again, he inexplicably passes on several opportunities to kill characters who will later play a part in his own undoing. The film also rehashes characters and situations from the original *Prophecy* to much lesser effect. Doe-eyed Brittany Murphy assumes the Renfield role played by Adam Goldberg and Amanda Plummer in the previous film. Eric Roberts, playing the Archangel Michael, appears to be under sedation.

Despite all its flaws, *Prophecy II* is worth renting to see an off-the-chain Walken once again dominate a film populated by lesser talents. It's like watching Mike Tyson beat the stuffing out of the skinny old man behind the neighborhood candy counter. Only bloodier. Walken and Hytner return for an improbable third episode two years later.

"Kids—they don't listen these days!"

—Gabriel, bemoaning the generation gap among evil archangels, in 1998's *The Prophecy II.*

PROPHECY 3: THE ASCENT   ★★

After two films as the scourge of mankind, Gabriel goes legit and helps save humanity from Pyriel, the Angel of Genocide, in the preposterous third installment of the *Prophecy* trilogy. Once again, the chase is on for Danyael the Nephilim, the half-man, half-angel spawn from 1998's *Prophecy II.* He's all grown up now and beset by his own weird religious visions. Gabriel, now a disheveled homeless man, reluctantly steps in as his guardian when the pursuing angel army gets too close.

Steve Hytner—who has either the best or the worst agent in Hollywood—returns yet again as Joseph the coroner, the caustic conscience of the *Prophecy* franchise. This time he has an even weightier role—or seems to, until his character inexplicably disappears halfway through the picture. That's just one of the many plot holes that have become hallmarks of the series. For instance, if this film is really set twenty years after the last one, why hasn't Hytner's character aged at all? How has he kept his job as a medical examiner after no fewer than five hermaphroditic angel corpses have either walked out of or been incinerated in his morgue over the course of three features? And why do the angels still rely on humans to drive them everywhere? Couldn't one of them have gotten a learner's permit in all that time between assaults on humanity?

These puzzlers wouldn't be nearly so bothersome if this film didn't lack the one thing that makes the *Prophecy* pictures worth watching—more Walken! Sad to say, he's barely in this one, and the switch to the good side of the Force doesn't serve his character well. This time, Walken ditches the **black** bob and the clown white face makeup for an ashen fright wig that makes him look like a Led Zeppelin roadie gone to seed. He has a few good lines, and one memorable encounter with a truckstop waitress from *Prophecy II*, but the celestial cowbells just aren't prominent enough. This remains by far the worst of three original *Prophecy* movies. (The series resumed, sans Walken in 2005, with *The Prophecy: Uprising*). Still, if you must have closure on the arc of Gabriel's character, it's worth a rental.

> *"Once I was the angel of death. Now I die every day—*
> *when I have the cash."*

—Gabriel the erstwhile Archangel, extolling the virtues of human prostitutes
in 2000's *Prophecy 3: The Ascent*

PULP FICTION   ★★★★

If you've been living in a cave since 1994, you might have missed this one, so here's the lowdown. Walken has only one scene in Quentin Tarantino's Oscar-nominated tale of logorrheic hitmen, redneck rapists, and a mysterious glowing briefcase. However, it includes one of the best speeches of his career, so you don't want to miss it. As Captain Koons, a Vietnam veteran, he explains the provenance of a very special gold watch to a little boy in a flashback sequence. The timepiece, which has been squirreled away in various characters' anal canals, will go on to play a critical role in the story. "It was great," Walken said of his quintessentially Tarantino-esque monologue. "I had the speech for months. I must say, in that case, every time I went through that long speech, every time I got to the end, it cracked me up. It stayed funny." Walken's work on *Pulp Fiction* took only half a

WALKEN PLAYS A GAME OF "HIDE THE WATCH" IN QUENTIN TARANTINO'S MASTERPIECE, *PULP FICTION*.

day, but it was time well spent. The film snagged seven Oscar nominations and helped re-establish Walken's hipster cred after a string of less than flattering choices in the early 1990s.

> *"I hid this uncomfortable hunk of metal up my ass two years. Then, after seven years, I was sent home to my family. And now, little man, I give the watch to you."*
>
> —Captain Koons, handing over the watch that takes a licking and keeps on ticking to a young Bruce Willis, in *Pulp Fiction*

PUNCTUATION

Punctuation is one of Walken's longtime pet peeves. He bristles at being told where to pause in a sentence, or what inflection to use. "I don't speak with punctuation," he says. "I remember my first encounter with punctuation: I resented it. I would never use commas or periods. . . . If I read a script and the sentence ends with a question, I'll almost always immediately make it a statement."

PUSS IN BOOTS   ★★★

Seventeen years after he helped Sean Connery pull off a high-stakes burglary in *The Anderson Tapes*, Walken played second banana to his son, Jason Connery, in this light-hearted musical adaptation of Charles Perrault's classic fairy tale. As the titular feline, Walken must help his master, a poor miller's son, win the hand of a beautiful princess played by Carmela Marner. Transformed into a human with the aid of a magical pair of boots, Walken gets to caper, stroke his moustache, and generally prance about in a catlike fashion—something that must have been a joy for him, given his love of **cats**. Indeed he was quite proud of his performance. "It's really one of my best movies," he observed of the 1988 release. "Nobody has ever seen this." Unfortunately, whenever Walken is off screen, the picture sags. *Puss in Boots* was one in a series of live-action fairy tales developed for the big screen under the Cannon Movie Tales umbrella.

> *"I had my hair dyed red, I had a moustache and I looked like a cat. It was very funny. It's a musical. I sing and dance in it. It's amazing what they do. No money. I didn't get paid anything."*
>
> —Walken, summarizing the appeal of one of his personal
> favorites, 1988's *Puss in Boots*

R

"RAVEN, THE"

Walken must have a special place in his heart for this Edgar Allan Poe chestnut. He recites part of the poem in the opening scene of 1983's *The Dead Zone*, and reads the entire thing on the 1997 all-celebrity Poe tribute CD *Closed on Account of Rabies*.

RAY, ALDO

This Italian-American actor of the **1950s** and 60s was a **childhood** hero of Walken's. The one-time U.S. Navy Frogman often appeared in war movies, which Walken and his friends would go see and then reenact in a vacant lot near their homes. Young Ronnie invariably played the Aldo Ray part: "I was sort of heroic, sure," Walken says. "I was never the bad guy. I was always gonna take that hill!"

RAZZIE

Walken has been nominated for three Golden Raspberry Awards for Worst Supporting Actor. In 2002, he became the second actor to be nominated for a Razzie and an Oscar in the same year, when the Golden Raspberry Award Foundation and the Motion Picture Association honored his work in *The Country Bears* and *Catch Me If You Can*, respectively. (James Coco had secured this dubious double honor in 1981; Alec Baldwin would duplicate it in 2003.) In 2003, Walken secured the coveted double Razzie nomination for his ghastly performances in *Gigli* and *Kangaroo Jack*.

> *"I do care. Very much. I care very much.*
> *I want to win them!"*
>
> —Walken, on his multiple Razzie nominations

RED EYE

Walken's home remedy for red eyes caused by lack of sleep is to soothe them with warm, wet tea bags.

REHEARSAL

Walken is a big proponent of rehearsals—especially on a movie shoot. "Rehearsal allows you to go home and sleep on it," he says. "If I'm shooting a scene with you next week, and the director says on your day off, let's go to the locations, go through the lines. It makes an enormous difference because you go home and you know where the door is, you know where the stove is, you know that you don't want the chair there, and a few days go by and even if it's subconsciously, you're working on it and it makes a huge difference."

RELIGION

Walken was raised a Methodist and professes a belief in the power of prayer. "God is very mysterious to me," he told *Parade* magazine in 1997, "but I know the power of belief. It's my source of strength." By his own admission, Walken went through a period in his young adulthood when he worshipped the moon for several years.

See also **Moon Worship**.

RIPPER

Following the lead of his *True Romance* **dance** partner Dennis Hopper, Walken tried his hand at acting in a video game in 1996. Set in a futuristic New York City, *Ripper* chronicles the hunt for a psychotic serial killer who disembowels his victims. Walken played Detective Vince Magnotta, the lawman assigned to the case. Burgess Meredith, Ossie Davis, Jimmie "J. J." Walker, and *Raiders of the Lost Ark*'s Karen Allen also appeared.

ROMANCE & CIGARETTES ★★★

Walken channels the spirit of his hero, **Elvis Presley**, to play a high-haired rockabilly goombah in this **musical** comedy fantasia from director John Turturro. Set in present day Queens, NY, the unusual film stars TV's Tony Soprano James Gandolfini as the improbably named Nick Murder, a chainsmoking outer borough lummox whose world comes crashing down after he cheats on his wife and gets lung cancer, in that order. The characters occasionally break out into song à la Walken's previous foray into movie **musicals**, *Pennies from Heaven*. Susan Sarandon plays Gandolfini's scorned wife, with Walken as her **Elvis**-obsessed Uncle Bo. Walken performs two songs: "Delilah" by Tom Jones and "Red Headed Woman" by Bruce Springsteen. Caught up in some studio squabbling, *Romance & Cigarettes* sat on the shelf for two years before getting a brief theatrical run in 2007.

"Some people fear the Lord. I fear women."

—Cousin Bo, sharing a little of his personal gospel, in 2007's *Romance & Cigarettes*

ROMEO AND JULIET

Walken absorbed some of the worst reviews of his career for his portrayal of Romeo at the Stratford **Shakespeare** Festival in 1968. He has called the performance "a disaster" and believes to this day that he only got the part because someone saw him wearing tights in *The Lion in Winter*. He has since had two more stabs at playing Romeo. "The second time I was better and the third time I was pretty good."

RONNIE

This familiar form of Walken's birth name, Ronald, is the moniker by which he's still known to his close friends and relatives.

WALKEN THROWS A PARTY IN THE COUNTY JAIL IN JOHN TURTURRO'S OUTER BOROUGH FANTASIA *ROMANCE & CIGARETTES*.

"I wasn't that comfortable with Ronnie. I don't know why. I didn't like the sound. Ronald, Donald, dorky."

—Walken, on his dissatisfaction with his birth name

ROSELAND   ★★

"I used to be prettier than I am," Walken has observed, "but I think I look better now. I was a pretty boy. Particularly in my early movies. I don't like looking at them so much. There's a sort of pretty thing about me." Nowhere is that observation more true than in this 1977 Merchant-Ivory production. Set in and around New York's legendary Roseland Ballroom, Roseland consists of three unrelated vignettes. Walken appears in the second one, "The Hustle," playing a young gigolo who becomes the object of a three-way catfight involving several older female admirers. It is one of several early, "sexy" roles that suggest he originally saw a future for himself as a romantic lead.

"I was really pretty—like a girl almost—and there was something narcissistic going on. I'm glad I got away from that. I guess I wanted to be a movie star. I'd have been better off if I'd just wanted to be an actor."

—Walken, on his early pretty boy persona

ROTC

Walken was briefly enrolled in the Reserve Officers Training Corps while attending Hofstra University in 1961.

ROUTINE

Walken is a creature of habit. "I do the same things every day," he says.

"I eat at the same time, I get up at the same time, I do the same things in the same order. I read. I have coffee. Then I study my scripts, I exercise on the treadmill, I make myself a little something to eat."

RUNDOWN, THE   ★★★

In another of his periodic attempts at playing an over-the-top supervillain (see *A View to a Kill* and *Batman Returns*), Walken strikes just the right antic note as Hatcher, the ruthless walking boss of an Amazon gold mine, in this 2003 action epic. Originally called *Helldorado*, *The Rundown* stars wrestler-turned-actor Dwayne "The Rock" Johnson as Beck, a musclebound bounty hunter who travels to South America to retrieve a gazillionaire's wayward son (*American Pie*'s Sean William Scott). Walken is the heartless tycoon who stands in his way. He hunts down his prey but is ultimately dispatched by his own bedraggled employees. The film is played mostly for laughs, with Walken given free rein to cackle maniacally, mug for the camera, and deliver several weird, Walkeny speeches that would sound ridiculous coming out of the mouth of any other actor. In one such monologue, Hatcher compares the disappearance of a priceless artifact to a little boy's being betrayed by the Tooth Fairy. In another, he spews venom at his Mestizo mine workers, calling them "oompah loompahs." (Reportedly, Walken was initially reluctant to speak this line, as he had never seen *Willy Wonka & the Chocolate Factory* before making this film.) A private park in Hawaii stood in for the Amazon rain forest— to the relief, no doubt, of Walken, who has vowed never again to make a movie in a **jungle**.

> *"Do you understand—the concept—of the Tooth Fairy?"*
>
> —Hatcher, unpacking a tortured metaphor for his befuddled minions, in 2003's *The Rundown*

WALKEN IS NO MATCH FOR AN ENRAGED DWAYNE
"THE ROCK" JOHNSON IN T*HE RUNDOWN*.

S to T

SARAH, PLAIN AND TALL ★★★

Fresh off two of the darkest, most flamboyant roles of his career—Frank White in *King of New York* and Robert in *The Comfort of Strangers*—Walken brought a different kind of intensity to his portrayal of a stoic Kansas widower in this 1991 Hallmark Hall of Fame TV movie. Based on Patricia MacLachlan's Newbery Medal–winning children's book, *Sarah, Plain and Tall* tells the tale of a mail-order bride from Maine who comes to live with a widowed farmer and his two young children in 1910. Glenn Close plays the titular consort, who helps Walken's emotionally bereft Jacob Witting deal with the grief caused by his wife's passing some years earlier. With his haunted gaze, rugged overalls, and goofy Caesar haircut, Walken looks like a cross between Buster Keaton and the farmer husband from Grant Wood's *American Gothic*. Nevertheless, he is quietly effective in the role, for which he received an Emmy nomination as Outstanding Lead Actor in a Miniseries or Special. Overall, *Sarah, Plain and Tall* notched nine Emmy nominations and spawned two sequels: *Skylark* and *Sarah, Plain and Tall: Winter's End*. Not bad for an unassuming family film that Glenn Close feared might end in bloodshed. "Everyone's going to think you're gonna murder us all in the end," she told Walken after he was cast against type in the fatherly role.

> *"What is right in my house is what I say is right!"*
>
> —Jacob Witting, laying down the law to his brand-new mail-order spouse in the *Hallmark Hall of Fame* production *Sarah, Plain and Tall*

SARAH, PLAIN AND TALL: WINTER'S END ★★

Shortly after making *Skylark*, the second film in the *Sarah, Plain and Tall* trilogy in 1993, Walken joked to an interviewer: "They're thinking about making a third one with my evil twin showing up. I could do

THE *SARAH, PLAIN AND TALL* TRILOGY INTRODUCED WALKEN TO
A WHOLE NEW AUDIENCE—TWELVE-YEAR-OLD FARMGIRLS.

one of those things where you play both roles." Sadly, the makers of *Sarah, Plain and Tall: Winter's End* didn't take him up on that creative suggestion. Instead they stick with the well-worn *Sarah, Plain and Tall* formula of heartfelt family drama, set against the forbidding landscape of Kansas circa 1918. Walken dons his bib overalls one last time as Jacob Witting, stolid patriarch of a prairie farming clan. This time around he must grapple with a whole new set of hardships in the form of his estranged father (Jack Palance), a broken leg, and the near-death from hypothermia of his beloved wife Sarah (Glenn Close). *Winter's End* is far and away the most tedious and least compelling of the *Sarah* films. Not surprisingly, it's the only one of the three not to receive any Emmy nominations. Walken is good as always, but a static plot and some truly terrible supporting performances undermine this effort from the start. The series had clearly shot its wad with 1993's vastly superior **Skylark**.

> *"Chris Walken says he'll only do it if they discover oil and move to Paris."*
>
> —executive producer William Self, on the prospects for a fourth installment in the *Sarah, Plain and Tall* series

SATURDAY NIGHT LIVE

Since 1990, Walken has been a recurring guest host on the late-night **television** sketch comedy show. In fact, he is one of a select group of guest hosts to be featured in his own *Saturday Night Live* "Best Of" DVD—an indication of the high regard in which he's held by the show's producer, Lorne Michaels. "He brings all his other castings and roles to his comedy," Michaels has said. "You see that face, and you associate it with lots of other things. So when he's playing light, he's that much more powerful . . . He's very funny."

From the outset, Walken made a strong impression on the

HIS MULTIPLE *SATURDAY NIGHT LIVE* APPEARANCES HELPED WALKEN
REBRAND HIMSELF AS A COMEDIC PERFORMER IN THE 1990s.

SNL cast as well. His first pitch session with the show's creative team resulted in a classic bit of Walken nonsense. The writers were throwing sketch ideas at him fast and furious. "You could be a carnival barker," said one. "You could be a **police** dispatcher," suggested another. Walken sat stone-faced throughout. Finally, Lorne Michaels asked him what kind of character he wanted to play. "Bear suits are funny," Walken deadpanned. "And bears as well." The bizarre non sequitur set the tone for all of Walken's subsequent appearances on the program. From then on, he would repeatedly be cast as a slightly dotty, somewhat affectless loon—most notably in the hilarious **census sketch** with Tim Meadows. Even greater fame would come, of course, with **the Continental** and the legendary **cowbell sketch**.

For Walken, hosting *SNL* has been a labor of love—and a reminder of his happy days as a child actor. "It's the place I'm most familiar with," he says of the program's Rockefeller Center studio. "When I go there to do *Saturday Night Live*, I'm walking down exactly the same halls I did as a child. There are many secret stairways and I know them all, the bathrooms have the same tiles. The door-knob into my dressing-room is the same as it was when I was a kid."

See also **Childhood** and *Ed Glosser: Trivial Psychic.*

SCAM   ★★★

Over the course of more than sixty films, screenwriters have come up with a lot of creative ways to try to do in Christopher Walken. He's been shot, stabbed, bludgeoned—even thrown off a blimp into the San Francisco Bay. In the 1993 Showtime Original Movie *Scam*, they try a nautical approach. Walken's character is subjected to the ancient sailor's punishment of keelhauling, but he lives to tell the tale and even exact revenge on his tormentors. That scene is just one of the many charms of this engaging noirish tale set in Miami and **Jamaica**. Walken plays Jack Shanks, a disgraced FBI agent posing as a con man posing as a mortician, who enlists the aid of a professional scam artist (Lorraine "Dr. Melfi" Bracco) in a scheme to bilk a ruth-less mobster out of his riches. Reggae star Maxi Priest provides the music and has a cameo as a Jamaican cab driver. As a charming rogue with a murderous, mercenary dark side, Walken gives one of his more underrated performances. He also goes shirtless in several scenes, a real treat for his legion of female admirers. We should all look so good the year we turn fifty.

TV'S DR. MELFI, LORRAINE BRACCO, PLAYS A GAME OF CAT AND MOUSE WITH WALKEN IN THE SHOWTIME ORIGINAL *SCAM*.

*"You mess with me, I'll come
down on you like a hammer."*

—Jack Shanks, spelling out the ground rules for his fellow grifter, Maggie Rohrer, in 1993's *Scam*

THINGS TO DO TO WALKEN TILL HE'S DEAD

You can't kill Christopher Walken . . . or can you? Here are some of
the innovative ways our hero has been dispatched on-screen over
the years. As you read, just keep telling yourself: it's only a movie,
it's only a movie . . .

- Leaps over a balcony to his death in **New Rose Hotel**
- Electrocuted in **Batman Returns**
- Has his heart ripped out by Lucifer in **The Prophecy**
- Falls off a blimp hovering above the Golden Gate Bridge in **A View to a Kill**
- Perishes in fiery van crash in **The Anderson Tapes**
- Blown away by his own brother in **The Funeral**
- Bludgeoned to death on the side of the road in **Search & Destroy**
- Blows his own brains out in **The Deer Hunter**
- Beheaded by two thousand-year-old embalmed Druid witch in **The Eternal**
- Beheaded by Nicole Kidman in **The Stepford Wives**
- Jumps off a building in **Mistress**
- Shot in the gut by vengeful mine workers in **The Rundown**

SCHNABEL, JULIAN

This American painter and filmmaker—and icon of the downtown
New York art scene of the 1980s—is one of Walken's closest friends.

A one-time short order cook, Schnabel encouraged Walken to launch a secondary career as a TV chef in the late 1990s. Together they appeared in the one-off Independent Film Channel production *Cooking with Chris* in 1999. In addition to **food**, the two men share a passion for **painting**. When Walken visits Schnabel, they occasionally work together on a canvas. "He threw a lot of paint down, and I danced around on it," Walken said of one such collaboration. "It was sort of interesting. It was red and green and blue and all that. It was a big mess, but it was an interesting mess."

SCOTLAND

"I feel very Scottish," Walken has said of his Highland ancestry. "I feel vestigial about it. I feel like a clansman. Tribal and warlike." Walken's mother came from a family of Scottish shipyard workers. She herself lived in Glasgow before she emigrated to New York. In 2000, Walken traveled to Glasgow to trace his family tree and visit his surviving Scottish relatives. "It was amazing," he says, "a lot of fun. I love Glasgow. It has a bad reputation, but all the best places and people have bad reputations." Describing his Scots relations as "interesting characters," Walken concluded: "I could happily live in Scotland and I don't mind being around our family." He also pines to work on the Glasgow stage, although union work rules make it difficult for him to do so.

SCOTLAND, PA   ★★

Walken plays against type as a persnickety homicide detective in this 2001 indie take-off on **Shakespeare's** *Macbeth*. As Detective Lieutenant Ernie McDuff, a strict vegetarian, Walken must put aside his distaste for meat long enough to unravel the mysterious death of the owner of a fast-food restaurant in the town of Scotland, Pennsylvania. The film's agreeable high concept is undermined by somewhat lackluster execution, although it's interesting to watch

MEAT REALLY IS MURDER IN THE 2001 "*MACBETH IN A HAMBURGER JOINT*" COMEDY *SCOTLAND, PA*

Walken's take on a Monk-like investigator. (Maybe there's a **television** series in his future?) He was attracted to the role—as he usually is—by the opportunity to do something different. "Christopher Walken told me he wanted to play a nice guy, because he's always been the bad guy," explained writer/director Billy Morrissette. Walken didn't mince words after receiving the screenplay: "[He] called me and said, 'It's a good script and I like the dialogue, but the ending is fucking stupid,'" Morrissette told *Movieline* magazine in 2002. "He scared the hell out of me. He didn't arrive until the twelfth day of filming, and I did not sleep until then. He had a zillion notes about what he wanted to change. I could see everybody watching me sweat. But he was actually really great and very funny."

SEARCH & DESTROY   ★★★

With *Wild Side*, *Things To Do in Denver When You're Dead*, and *The Prophecy*, Walken was clearly on a mission in 1995, seemingly determined to cram as many bizarre characters as possible into one calendar year. Kim Ulander, the sleazy, homicidal businessman he plays in this dark satire, is one of his more subdued creations during this period, but a memorable one nonetheless. Directed by visual artist David Salle and based on a stage play by Howard Korder, *Search & Destroy* chronicles the travails of a tax cheat (Griffin Dunne) who dreams of making a big score in the movie business with a little help from some ill-gotten seed money supplied by Walken's character. In one of the film's more inspired scenes, Walken and Dunne visit a Japanese restaurant, where Walken performs a karaoke rendition of the classic folk song "Red River Valley," complete with tap dance accompaniment. Also on hand is frequent Walken co-conspirator John Turturro, who delivers a madcap performance as a bewigged loon who went to college (**Hofstra University**, it just so happens) with Walken's character. He now has a sideline in fraudulent credit cards. (Their close friendship doesn't prevent Walken from shooting him, however, for no apparent reason.) Ileana Douglas and Dennis Hopper also star. The film is uneven, and it takes some strange dark turns that seem to come out of nowhere. Truth be told, the pace sags whenever Walken and Turturro are off screen. But their chemistry is so good, and they are so clearly enjoying their byplay, that it's worth checking out just to envision what kind of comedy team they would make in a parallel universe.

"You can't have an adventure without a gun!"

—Kim Ulander, sharing some of his life wisdom with Griffin Dunne's moviemaking
nebbish, Martin Mirkheim, in 1995's *Search & Destroy*

SENTINEL, THE ★

The box office success of *The Exorcist* inspired a host of inferior imitations. Some, like *The Omen*, were good, grisly fun. Others, like this 1977 oddity from *Death Wish* director Michael Winner, were abominations unto the god of cinema. *The Sentinel* may not be the worst horror movie ever made, but it is easily the most incomprehensible. Set in Brooklyn, the convoluted plot concerns an old, blind priest (a waxwork John Carradine) who guards the mouth of Hell within the walls of his tastefully appointed brownstone apartment. Christina Raines plays the unfortunate woman who moves in downstairs. Walken has a tiny, thankless role as Rizzo, a cop who investigates the weird goings-on. He is on screen for all of five minutes, for which he should be eternally grateful. This film all but killed the once-promising career of Chris Sarandon. If Walken had been in it any longer, he may have become a casualty as well. A host of C-list stars are on hand to keep things moving, including Burgess Meredith as an elderly queen with a parakeet on his shoulder; Sylvia Miles and Beverly D'Angelo as a pair of lesbian cannibals; and a decrepit Ava Gardner as a snooty realtor. The gruesome finale involves buckets of spurting blood and an army of real-life circus freaks. Thankfully, Walken is long gone by then. Rent at your own risk.

SHAKESPEARE

Walken has had his ups and downs as a Shakespearean actor. He won plaudits for his work in *Coriolanus* and *Measure for Measure*, but puzzled many critics with space alien performances in *Romeo and Juliet* and *Othello*. John Lazarus, a Canadian playwright and professor at Queen's University in Canada, recalls seeing the young Walken play Lysander in *A Midsummer-Night's Dream* at the 1968 Stratford **Shakespeare** Festival. "I actually didn't think he was particularly good. I remember him delivering the first joke in the play—'You have her father's love, Demetrius; let me have Hermia's: do you marry him'— straight out to the audience, in a way that struck me as phony."

Walken himself has conceded the ragged nature of some of his Shakespearean work. "I remember I played *Richard II* once and people came backstage and they would say, 'Loved your *Hamlet*,'" he jokes. The one dream role he's yet to play? That other Richard, the hunchbacked villain. Says Walken: "I don't think I would have to act much if I played *Richard III*."

> **"Shakespeare has survived worse actors than me. I'm not going to put a dent in his reputation."**
>
> —Walken, to the *New York Times* in 1982

SHOOT THE SUN DOWN ★★

"Into the sands, one man rode alone," blared the publicity copy for this ponderous 1978 western. That man is Walken, who doesn't even attempt to conceal his thick New York accent as the enigmatic Mr. Rainbow, a samurai-like loner whose weapon of choice is a ninja throwing star. Set on America's Mexican frontier in 1836, *Shoot the Sun Down* chronicles Mr. Rainbow's encounter with an unscrupulous gold prospector (Bo Brundin) and his indentured female companion (Margot Kidder). The film moves at a snail's pace, with little or no action until the final reel, when Walken's character is tied down on the desert sands and pecked at by vultures before escaping and precipitating a climactic confrontation. It's also painfully derivative—with Mr. Rainbow clearly modeled on

Clint Eastwood's Man with No Name and a visual style borrowed from Akira Kurosawa. Still, it's worth a look to see Walken loping about the New Mexico desert on a slow horse, gazing portentously at passersby. (Interestingly enough, the character was originally supposed to be out-fitted with rainbow-tinted sunglasses—hence his ludicrous surname—but director David Leeds scrapped that idea the first time he saw Walken wearing them. "They just looked weird, not cool or believable at all.")

Although it wasn't released until 1978, *Shoot the Sun Down* was actually filmed over six weeks in August and September 1976, in the desert outside of Santa Fe and at the White Sands missile testing range in New Mexico. The shoot was arduous, particularly for Walken, who insisted on really being tied down for the "pecked by vultures" sequence. According to Leeds, he refused to let himself be untied even when the production broke for lunch. The vultures, who were secured in place with wire, grew frantic and broke away from their restraints on several occasions. They attacked the helpless Walken but fortunately did not damage his face.

While it makes for an interesting curiosity when viewed today, *Shoot the Sun Down* seemed like an odd choice for Walken at the time it was made. The material seems ill-suited to his persona, a fact he may have been alluding to when he complained about his handlers in a 1981 interview: "I had press agents that a studio hired doing ridiculous things that I didn't find out about until later. I got rid of them immediately. They were trying to sell me as the new Clint Eastwood. He's very good—I like him—but he's got it all tied up. I don't want to be that. I want to be something else." Perhaps singed by the *Shoot the Sun Down* experience, Walken would rarely return to the western genre. He offered a very different take on the laconic gunman icon two years later in *Heaven's Gate*.

SILENT FILMS

With his haunted gaze and deep-set features, Walken would have
made an expressive silent film star in the mold of Buster Keaton. He
agrees. "I'd love to be a silent movie actor," he once remarked. "If I
had a day in movies where I get on the horse, come to town, tie up
horse, come out, shovel some hay, that would be great."

See also **Horses.**

SKYLARK   ★★★

There's a drought ravaging the prairie, Glenn Close's biological clock
is ticking, and the only cure is more Walken in this 1993 sequel to

WALKEN RETURNED TO THE PRAIRIE FOR MORE
MAUDLIN FAMILY DRAMA IN 1993's *SKYLARK*.

1991's *Sarah, Plain and Tall*. Skylark once again chronicles the travails of the Witting family as they try to make a go of farming in 1912 Kansas. This time, they are beset by a host of new plagues, including the aforementioned drought, Sarah's feelings of homesickness, and a fire that destroys their barn. Despite all the hardships, Walken's character, Jacob Witting, isn't as tightly wound in this installment. He gets to smile more, and he dances with Glenn Close's Sarah under the moonlight. At one point, he even helps birth a calf. It's a heartfelt follow-up to the acclaimed *Sarah, Plain and Tall* that earned Close a second Emmy nomination for her performance, and *Sarah, Plain and Tall: Winter's End* rounded out the trilogy six years later.

SLEEPY HOLLOW   ★★★

Sixteen years after he read "The Legend of Sleepy Hollow" to his English class as Johnny Smith in *The Dead Zone*, Walken got the chance to play The Headless Horseman in this 1999 big-screen adaptation of Washington Irving's classic story. Directed by Walken's old *Batman Returns* confrère Tim Burton, *Sleepy Hollow* stars Johnny Depp as Ichabod Crane, the hapless constable sent to investigate a series of mysterious decapitations in an upstate New York town. As the headless grotesque, Walken delivers a powerful, wordless performance—complete with feral grunts and bared fangs. He claims to have modeled his characterization on Lon Chaney Jr.'s portrayal of The Wolf Man in the Universal horror films of the 1940s.

SMALLS, BIGGIE

The late hip-hop superstar also known as The Notorious B.I.G. (real name: Christopher Wallace) was a huge **fan** of Walken. He occasionally styled himself as "the black Frank White" in honor of Walken's gangster character in *King of New York*. In 1997, the two icons

NOT YET HEADLESS, THE HESSIAN HORSEMAN BARES
HIS FANGS IN TIM BURTON'S *SLEEPY HOLLOW*.

almost met. According to one of Smalls's associates, Damion
"D-Roc" Butler, Walken called Smalls' hotel room while Biggie was
in California shooting the video for "Hypnotize." "Walken called
Big's room and said, 'This is Frank White,'" Butler reported. "Big was

like, 'Yeah, right,' and hung up the phone. Big thought he was playin'
since Frank White was also his little nickname. And then [Walken]
called back like, 'No, I'm serious. I'm Christopher Walken and I'd like
to come meet you.' Big was so happy, but they never met."

SPACEY, KEVIN

The man whom Walken's own wife believes does the best **impression** was a reluctant convert to the craft of Walken imposture.
Spacey has admitted that he never "did" Walken before his cele-
brated January 1997 appearance on *Saturday Night Live*. During
that show, he performed a spot-on impression of Walken auditioning for the part on **Han Solo** in *Star Wars*. "I was sitting around
with the writers, asking them about previous hosts," Spacey
recalled. "Who was drunk, who was a pain in the ass? They told me
about Christopher Walken. One of them said, 'Remember when he
talked about auditioning for *Star Wars*?' I never knew he had."
Intrigued, Spacey asked some friends to teach him how to do a
Walken impression. He supplemented his study by watching several
Walken movies. The hard work paid off. Although Spacey himself
calls his Walken impersonation only "passable," his friends still resent
the acclaim he receives for getting his version on the air first. "They
wanted to burn me alive," Spacey says, "because they'd been working on it for years. I come along and do the *Reader's Digest* version,
and I get all the attention."

SPORTS

Walken is not a sports fan and claims he's never attended a baseball
game in his life. Even as a child growing up in **Astoria**, Queens, he was
more interested in acting out scenes from **Aldo Ray** movies on the
playground than shooting hoops. "I remember there was this concrete
place and somebody at one point put a basketball hoop up," the actor

once recalled. "I remember standing with my friends, and we stared at it like it was a flying saucer. 'What are we supposed to do?'"

Although he may not play himself, Walken looks to athletes for inspiration and claims **Muhammad Ali** as one of his heroes. "I'm very interested in athletes," he has said.

> I find I always learn something about acting when I watch them. It has to do with the focus of their minds—control, you know. The idea of having to do what you do within a very small period of time—and preparing yourself for that moment. And being so much in control that thought about it vanishes. One just does it.

STAGE DIRECTIONS

One of Walken's pet peeves in a script is the excessive use of stage directions. "I've read scripts where the stage directions were like an operator's manual like when you buy a washing machine. I don't look at them. I don't pay any attention to anything but the dialogue. If a line comes with the direction 'wistfully' or 'angrily,' it makes me want to do the opposite."

STAND-UP COMEDY

Walken has admitted the idea of performing comedy on stage is "kind of a fantasy of mine." One can only hope that, like his dream of a **cooking** show, this fantasy will one day become a reality. "I think I could do it, actually. It might almost be funnier, because people wouldn't expect it. But I think I could do that. A sort of Rodney Dangerfield thing."

STAR WARS: EPISODE II—ATTACK OF THE CLONES

In the summer of 2000, rumors began to circulate on the Internet that Walken would play an evil Sith Lord named Darth Bane in the then-forthcoming *Star Wars* epic *Attack of the Clones*. The whispers originated with an erroneous post on Harry Knowles's *Ain't It Cool News* website. At one point even Walken himself started to wonder whether the story was true. "I even asked," he said. "I said maybe I am in it and they're saving it for a surprise. But I'm not in that movie and I never was. I don't know how that happened."

THE STEPFORD WIVES   ★

Not content with appearing in two of the most accursed big-budget bombs of all time (see *Gigli* and *Heaven's Gate*, respectively), Walken went for the trifecta with this ill-starred comedy remake of a 1975 horror movie, loosely based on Ira Levin's 1972 novel. He plays Mike Wellington, the de facto burgermeister of a tweedy Connecticut town where all the **women** have been replaced by cheery, bodacious, eerily efficient robots—much to the delight of their trollish husbands. Surrounding Walken—and seemingly searching for the life rafts from the opening frame—were such accomplished actors as Matthew Broderick, Glenn Close, Bette Midler, and Nicole Kidman. Aside from the film's general awfulness, there are two aesthetic oddities worth noting. Walken wears his **hair** styled in a manner that evokes a late-model Jerry Stiller and, at least for a portion of the film, a corset. "I wore the girdle for a few days and it was fine," he told Conan O'Brien, "but then they said the girdle doesn't matter, you can take it off, so I did for a few days, but I felt I needed it, so I put it back on and I wore it through the whole movie, and it was kind of my character."

The Stepford Wives was pilloried in the press from the moment

WALKEN AND GLENN CLOSE MAY HAVE BEEN ALL SMILES, BUT RUMORS OF ACRIM
AMONG THE CAST PLAGUED THE MISBEGOTTEN REMAKE OF *THE STEPFORD WIVI*

shooting started, with rumors abounding of tension on the set and hastily ordered rewrites to screenwriter Paul Rudnick's already dreadful script. Reportedly, the all-star cast did not mesh. "They were at each others' throats," one on-set informant told the *New York Post*. Walken denied the rumors, calling them "mysterious." The backstage atmosphere, he said, "was really like a playground every day, all those terrific actors. We played and got paid for it. I would love to make another movie with that whole bunch of people." One point of conflict that no one disputes concerned the film's ending. Appalled that a late rewrite had his character revealed to be a robot and decapitated with a candelabrum, Walken raised holy hell to producer Scott Rudin. Rudin prevailed. The crew then spent three weeks of filming with a dummy standing in for Walken's dead body. Rudin later played down talk of a rift, saying: "I have enjoyed working with Christopher Walken before, and I have enjoyed working with him now. Hopefully I can work with him in the future."

If he did walk off the set, at least Walken didn't have very far to go. Many of the exterior scenes were shot about ten minutes from his home in Connecticut, making for an easy commute. Interiors were shot it in the Kaufman Studios in **Astoria**, about three blocks from the place where Walken was born. "I was within a few blocks of the place where I took my tap-dancing lessons," he revealed. "And that neighborhood hasn't really changed much, so I was walking around on streets that were very familiar to me. . . . That was an ideal situation." It's nice to know that someone has pleasant memories associated with this film.

"I looked like Victor Mature."

—Walken, on the strange look of his character, Mike Wellington, in the 2004 turkey *The Stepford Wives*

STREETCAR NAMED DESIRE, A

In the 1982 **television** film *Who Am I This Time?*, in which he plays a small-town stage actor, Walken gave audiences a glimpse of how he might take on Stanley Kowalski, the brutish lummox at the center of Tennessee Williams' Pulitzer Prize–winning play. Four years later, in Williamstown, Massachusetts, he took the plunge for real. In the eyes of most critics, the results weren't pretty. "While enhancing his role with a swaggering humor, Mr. Walken sacrifices a measure of

Stanley's menace," wrote Mel Gussow in the *New York Times*. "An additional difficulty is the actor's physical appearance; his bared torso physique does not seem convincingly Stanley-like." Ouch. These days, Walken shrugs off the bad reviews, claiming he played Stanley strictly for laughs. "It was a stitch," he says, "but a lot of people criticized me for doing that. But what the fuck was I supposed to do? I never was Stanley to begin with."

STUDIO 54

In the late 1970s, Walken was a regular denizen of the famed New York City discotheque. But the allure of the mirror ball quickly faded. He moved on, saying: "There comes a time when you're out there on the disco floor and you feel foolish."

See also **Dancing.**

SUGAR

This sweetener is one white powder from which Walken religiously abstains. "I don't do sugar. It has a chemical effect on me. There are very few things that get me tense. I can drink a lot of coffee. But if I have half a soda I get wired."

SUICIDE KINGS   ★★

Walken has his finger cut off about ten minutes into this Tarantino-esque 1997 feature about a kidnapping plot perpetrated by a gaggle of in-over-their-head preppies. As Carlo Bartolucci, a John Gotti type mob boss who plays an extended cat-and-mouse game with his abductors, Walken spends most of the movie confined to a chair, bound with duct tape. The role presented him with an interesting physical challenge. "When I read the script, all the darker aspects aside, it was about a man my age who was put into this experience of having to save himself with his mind. I'm a physical actor, and I'm strapped to a chair, so

ADDING ANOTHER CHARACTER TO HIS ROGUE'S GALLERY, WALKEN
PLAYS A RESOURCEFUL MOBSTER IN 1997'S *SUICIDE KINGS*.

I had to really think about what I was talking about very carefully. . . .
It's a more human story than I usually get to play." The one drawback
of his character's immobility was being unable to throw in one of his
signature musical flourishes. "I wasn't able to tap dance, you know?
Maybe it's the only movie that I never danced in."

Suicide Kings also gave Walken the opportunity to work with Jay
Mohr, his old *Saturday Night Live* confrère and one of the world's
premier Walken impressionists. "Jay used to do me on the set. He
would do me playing my part for the movie. I ended up imitating
Jay's impersonation of me for my role." A lot of Walken's dialogue
was improvised, according to costar Johnny Galecki:

> [Walken] likes to kind of think aloud and lets you know
> where his thoughts are and where he's at in a scene either

mentally or emotionally and lets you know where he's going with it. A lot of those thoughts that he spoke aloud became lines and were left in the movie and gave us the freedom to do the same. In every scene there is some ad-libbing at the very least.

> *"Anybody wants to hold hands with my dick, I insist they buy me a drink first."*
>
> —Carlo Bartolucci, to his kidnappers, in *Suicide Kings*

SWEET BIRD OF YOUTH

In one of the finest stage performances of his career, Walken played Chance Wayne, a stud gone to seed, in the 1975 Broadway revival of Tennessee Williams's 1959 play. Irene Worth played Princess Kosmonopolis, the faded movie actress who falls prey to Chance's charms. Critics were charmed as well. "Both Miss Worth and Mr. Walken are superb," wrote Clive Barnes of the *New York Times*. Walken had, he said, "a kind of beauty to him but he invests it with a decadence that recalls Baudelaire and other doomed souls." Writing in the same paper, Walter Kerr called Walken's Chance "far and away his best work since his Caligula at Yale." And the *Nation*'s Harold Clurman observed, "There is in everything he does a cold, energetic resentment with a strong admixture of superciliousness that fits the part all too well." Apparently, critics weren't the only ones swooning over Walken's charismatic gigolo. The play's director, Edwin Sherin, noticed Walken's performance fogging the glasses of some of the other members of the company. "The way he handled his body in *Sweet Bird* turned everybody on," Sherrin said. "The girls with the production were affected by it, and so were a lot of the fellows, consciously or otherwise."

Irene Worth was another member of Walken's burgeoning fan club. When the play's New York run ended, it was scheduled to open again in London with a new actor in the lead. But Worth was so transfixed by Walken's performance she refused to take the stage with anybody else playing Chance. For Walken, the good feeling was mutual. "I learned more acting in the theater with Irene Worth in *Sweet Bird of Youth* than I could have learned from ten years in acting school," he said of the experience. The intense portrayal did take a personal toll on him, however. He has admitted to drinking heavily during the play's run. "The roughest time I ever had was playing that guy," Walken said later. "He was such a loser, so pathetic and yet so likable. I found it affected me deeply. I became sort of a loser myself."

TELEVISION

Walken is not an avid television viewer. (He says he has never seen a single episode of *Seinfeld* or *South Park*, for instance.) He does have a few favorite shows. He likes to doze off to *The Honeymooners* or *The Odd Couple*, has admitted to being a fan of the **Food Network** staple *Iron Chef*, and says he enjoys watching stand-up comics perform on Comedy Central. Generally speaking, however, he only watches two things on TV with any regularity: *Charlie Rose* and movies. "I have fifty or sixty movie channels on satellite," Walken told *FilmStew* magazine. "I surf for movies, that's mostly what I do. And I always stop if I see the one I'm in." The results can be gratifying—or mortifying, depending on what mood he's in and what movie he stumbles across. "Sometimes I see something that I did ten years ago that I thought I was awful in, and I wasn't that bad." Other times, Walken says, he finds himself critiquing his own performance. "I think, Chris, don't let your mouth hang open like that next time. Look at that facial tic. Don't walk in such a self-conscious way! But sometimes, I watch myself and

I think that I am terrific—and that is really nice."

> *"When I don't have any work sometimes, a kind of thing sets in where my mind shuts down. It's almost like hibernation. It's not that I'm unhappy, but I'm not thinking anything. Then I'll go and watch television. And after an hour or two, I'll think, 'You're just sitting there watching television and it's not even interesting.' And there's nothing to do. Life becomes meaningless."*

—Walken, on the stultifying power of television

THINGS TO DO IN DENVER WHEN YOU'RE DEAD   ★★★

"Take out my dick . . . Take it OUT!!!" With those words, Walken adds yet another unforgettable villain to his cinematic pantheon. As a creepy paraplegic crime lord who glides around his shadowy grotto in a motorized wheelchair issuing racist and homophobic pronouncements, he all but steals the picture from its star, Andy Garcia. Unfortunately, it's not a picture worth stealing. A title in search of a premise (the title is actually derived from an obscure Warren Zevon song, which the songwriter refused to provide for the film's soundtrack), *Things to Do in Denver When You're Dead* is a Quentin Tarantino-inspired jumble about an underworld goon gone straight (Garcia) who runs afoul of the local mob boss (Walken) with gruesomely violent consequences. Steve Buscemi plays a fearsome hit man, with Treat Williams and *Taxi*'s Christopher Lloyd as members of Garcia's crew. In one of many too-clever-for-its-own-good touches, Walken's character is inexplicably referred to only as "The Man with the Plan"—although presumably he has a name. Having turned down parts in *Reservoir Dogs* and *The Usual Suspects*, it's strange that

THE ABSURDLY NAMED "MAN WITH THE PLAN," WALKEN CALLS THE SHOTS FROM HIS MOTORIZED WHEELCHAIR IN *THINGS TO DO IN DENVER WHEN YOU'RE DEAD.*

Walken would accept a role in this derivative mishmash, which borrows elements from both of those pictures. He makes the most of his time on screen, however, ordering about his buxom female attendants with barely concealed glee, and doing a lot of hollow-eyed staring.

It was the first of two roles in a two-year span requiring Walken to act around physical confinement. (He plays a man tied to a chair in 1997's *Suicide Kings*.) "In a way, that was difficult," Walken says, "but in another way it frees you from having to make a lot of choices." Walken's commitment to the part impressed the rest of the creative team. "He's sitting there—a head," raved *Denver* director Gary Fleder. "How many guys out there can do that? Nicholson can do it. Probably Pacino. And then Chris Walken's a guy who can do it time and time again. You can just sit and watch him speak." "He really out-Walkens Walken," added screenwriter Scott Rosenberg. "He's just so out there."

So out there, in fact, that he scared even his own friends. After *Denver*'s release, Walken told a story about taking a buddy of his to see the film in a theater. Afterwards, Walken noticed a look of abject horror on his friend's face. "Jesus Christ," the friend said, "that's the most terrible person I ever saw. . . . That's just the most terrible person I ever saw." Walken thanked him for the compliment and they went their separate ways.

> *"I'm a criminal. My word don't mean dick!"*
>
> —The Man with the Plan, engaging in a little post hoc justification for yet another brutal hit, in 1995's *Things to Do in Denver When You're Dead*

THREE LITTLE PIGS, THE

In one of his more entertaining talk show appearances, Walken read this classic fairy tale during a 1993 visit to British chatmeister Jonathan Ross's *Saturday Zoo*. Seated in an enormous chair, and wearing a garish floral sweater that looked as if he'd rescued it from Dr. Clifford Huxtable's discard pile, Walken recited the story from an oversized book of fairy tales in a heavy New York accent, with characteristically Walkenesque flourishes ("Arrividerci, porco numero due. Buon giorno, salami.") Asked to explain his performance, Walken said only: "I frequently do things like that. I thought it was amusing."

TOUCH   ★★

In the mid-1990s, Walken carved out a new niche for himself playing sleazy con men and slick operators. (See *A Business Affair*, *Scam*, and *Search & Destroy* for other examples.) This lightweight 1997 comedy, Walken's second feature for director Paul Schrader, caps off that string of performances. Adapted from a novel by Elmore Leonard, *Touch* tells the story of Juvenal (Skeet Ulrich), a stigmatic hottie who can heal people with the touch of his hand. Walken plays Bill Hill, an unscrupulous ex-evangelist who plots to cash in on Juvenal's miracle work. The unusual cast includes Tom Arnold as a local religious fanatic, Janeane Garofalo as a nosy newspaperwoman, and a woefully miscast Paul Mazursky as a fast-talking record promoter. Don Novello—Father Guido Sarducci from *Saturday Night Live*—has a brief cameo as an aggrieved priest. The film can't seem to make up its mind whether it wants to be a broad satire or a heartfelt meditation on religious faith. However, it's pleasant enough to merit a looksee if you're a Walken completist. One interesting anecdote from the set: Skeet Ulrich came upon a religious term in the script he didn't understand. When he asked Walken about it, Walken gave him the following advice: "You know, other actors, they'd look that up. I just say it. I don't care what it is." "The genius of Chris Walken," Ulrich concluded. "Of course, I think he was lying. I think he's a complete preparer."

TROILUS AND CRESSIDA

In another of his periodic Shakespearean misfires, Walken played

WALKEN PRAISES THE LORD WITH HIS BLING IN PAUL SCHRADER'S *TOUCH*.

Prince Achilles—the arrogant, cowardly Greek warrior—as a simpering dolt in a spotted feather boa in this 1973 New York Shakespeare Festival production of the Bard's 1602 tragedy. Critics savaged the unconventional production, reserving special contempt for Walken's performance. "Mr. Walken is asked to read 'My reputation is at stake,' as though he'd just come out of *The Godfather*," wrote Walter Kerr in the *New York Times*. He also faulted Walken for delivering some of his lines in a Puerto Rican accent. Of the feather boa, Kerr wrote, it made him look "rather like Tarzan with seaweed."

TRUE ROMANCE   ★★★★

This hyperkinetic 1993 "lovers on the lam" epic from director Tony Scott helped launch the career of Quentin Tarantino, who used the money he got from writing this script to help finance his directorial debut, *Reservoir Dogs*. For Walken watchers, however, *True Romance* is perhaps best known for the so-called "Sicilian scene," the verbal *pas de deux* between Walken and Dennis Hopper that jump starts the film's third act. The exchange takes place in a dingy trailer between mobster Vincenzo Coccotti (Walken) and security guard Clifford Worley (Hopper). Worley's son has some narcotics that belong to Coccotti, and Coccotti, in a roundabout speech that begins with declaring himself "the antichrist" and grows more ominous from there, tries to convince Worley to give up his boy's whereabouts. Not surprisingly, the scene ends with a hail of gunfire—this is a Tarantino movie, after all.

The dialogue is superb, but it's the byplay between the two actors that elevates the scene to another level. People often assume the scene was improvised, but Walken and Hopper actually stuck pretty closely to what Tarantino had written. "Every word was scripted," Walken says. "That's the way Quentin Tarantino writes, like a play—big speeches." The scene was shot in two takes—one on Hopper, one on Walken. When they got to the part where Hopper

WALKEN AND DENNIS HOPPER DISCUSS EGGPLANTS—AND
OTHER MATTERS—IN TONY SCOTT'S *TRUE ROMANCE.*

likens Walken to a Sicilian eggplant, the actors could barely contain
their glee. "He started telling that story and I started to laugh off camera," Walken says. "Then when they turned it around and shot me and
we got to the same place, I started to laugh again and he started to
laugh. It was like in school when you can't stop laughing and the
teacher's mad at you." Hopper also noted the fortuitous synergy
between the two performers. "We got in a zone, as they say now in
sports," he says, "where we were really living in our subconscious in
a moment-to-moment reality."

HAVEN'T KILLED ANYBODY SINCE 1984." *TRUE ROMANCE*'S VINCENZO COCCOTTI
IS ONE OF WALKEN'S EFFECTIVE ONE-SCENE PERFORMANCES.

Widely disseminated via Web video, the Sicilian scene has attained cult status among actors, film geeks, and Tarantinophiles. Walken's close friend Sean Penn calls it "the best pop-culture scene ever shot. . . . The hostility buried under the hopelessness of those guys . . . it's very clear what's going to happen from the beginning, and yet you're tortured in waiting, because both actors draw it out." Tarantino himself called it "one of the best scenes I've ever seen in my life . . . and that has nothing to do with what I wrote."

> *"It was delightful, don't you think? It happens to end with me shooting him in the head. But up until then, wasn't it delightful?"*
>
> —Walken, on the celebrated "Sicilian Scene" in *True Romance*

TUPPERWARE

Walken is an avid collector of the revolutionary kitchen storage products.

U TO V

UNDERTAKING BETTY   ★★

Walken plays a boorish American mortician who wants to "put the fun back in funerals" in this twee British comedy from 2002. Also known as *Plots with a View*, the film chronicles the rivalry between small-town Welsh undertaker Boris Plots (Alfred Molina) and Milwaukee-born interloper Frank Featherbed (Walken, sporting an enormous Monty Python wig). In his effort to steal business from his competitor, Walken's character stages a number of elaborately themed wakes—including one where he tap dances in front of the casket and another where he dresses up as Mr. Spock from *Star Trek*. The far-fetched mortuary farce is intermittently charming in the manner of *The Full Monty* or *Four Weddings and a Funeral*—but with more funerals. For Walken completists only.

USUAL SUSPECTS, THE

Reportedly, Walken turned down the role of U.S. Customs Agent Dave Kujan in the 1995 thriller. Robert De Niro and Al Pacino also passed on the part, which went to Chazz Palminteri. Had he taken it, *The Usual Suspects* would have given Walken the chance to appear on screen alongside two of his best-known celebrity impersonators: **Kevin Spacey** and Kevin Pollak.

VALLEY FORGE   ★★

"I could get away with being a German commandant and not really have to do a lot of accent," Walken observed in 2000, "because I already sound like I don't speak English that well." In this early television appearance, he was already putting that theory to the test. A December 1975 TV movie that aired under the banner of the Hallmark Hall of Fame, playwright Maxwell Anderson's *Valley Forge* retells the dramatic story of George Washington's army and its winter of discontent in upstate New York. Walken has one scene, playing

a German officer identified only as "The Hessian," whose support the
colonial army attempts to enlist. Described by another character as "a
feckless, stateless, wandering mercenary," Walken is suitably shifty as
he sips brandy and compliments the American generals on the quality of their poultry. True to his word, he attempts only the barest of
German accents. It was his second Hallmark Hall of Fame appearance. (He had previously played Lamprocles, son of Socrates, in a
1966 production of *Barefoot in Athens*.) Richard Basehart plays
George Washington, with Victor Garber as General Lafayette. The
New York Times called *Valley Forge* "one of the more successful addi-
tions to the Bicentennial hopper."

> *"You're most hospitable hosts. The chicken was most*
> *lovely . . . so fat."*
>
> —The Hessian, complimenting his American counterparts on a bird well cooked, in
> 1975's *Valley Forge*

VAN VOOREN, MONIQUE

This buxom Belgian actress, model, and nightclub performer convinced **Ronnie** Walken to change his stage name to **Christopher**. An
eye-popping fixture of print ads of the **1950s** and 60s, Van Vooren left
a lasting impression on young Walken, who was one of her backup
dancers. "She was so gorgeous," Walken remembers. "Really hot, let's
face it, that's the word. She had that European thing." In 1983, Van
Vooren pled guilty to perjury after she was charged with stealing her
late mother's Social Security payments.

VENDETTA   ★★

Old New Orleans provides the setting for this fact-based HBO
drama about one of the most notorious lynchings in American his-

tory. Walken plays James Houston, a diabolical cotton magnate who concocts a scheme to wrest control from the "eyetalian" immigrants who run the city's docks. He frames a ragtag group of "degos" for the murder of the chief of police, and incites mob violence when the ensuing trial exonerates the accused men. There is much moustache twirling, bourbon sipping, and cigar puffing throughout.

VIEW TO A KILL, A   ★

When he looks back on his long career, Walken can claim the distinction of having played the villain in the worst **James Bond** movie ever made. A thinly disguised rehash of *Goldfinger*, *A View to a Kill* (1985) manages to make its lackluster predecessor—the execrably titled *Octopussy*—look like a cinematic masterpiece by comparison. The incoherent plot has Bond investigating an attempt to destroy Silicon Valley with a massive earthquake, thereby winnowing down the world's supply of microchips. Sporting a ludicrous blonde dye job (in a role originally intended for David Bowie), Walken sleepwalks through his performance as Max Zorin, the wealthy French industrialist who concocts the insane scheme. Nazi steroid experiments have supposedly turned Zorin into a super genius, but nothing he says or does over the course of this interminable 131-minute film indicates he possesses anything like an above-average intellect. The action scenes, including a climactic confrontation on Zorin's zeppelin hovering above the Golden Gate Bridge, are flaccid and uninvolving. A chase through the streets of San Francisco on a fire engine plays like something out of an Abbott and Costello movie. In his final go-round as 007, Roger Moore looks old and tired. The rest of the cast is abominable. Supermodel Grace Jones, as Zorin's henchwoman May Day, and former Charlie's Angel Tanya Roberts, as a geologist who runs afoul of the psychotic tycoon, give amateurish performances that bespeak their lack of acting experience.

WALKEN AND GRACE JONES PROVE TO BE NO MATCH FOR A GERIATRIC
ROGER MOORE IN THE JAMES BOND EPIC *A VIEW TO A KILL*.

More than twenty years later, it's still unclear why Walken took part in this catastrophe, which came right on the heels of his well-received performance in *The Dead Zone*. (He remains the most accomplished actor ever to take on the role of a **James Bond** villain.) One clue may lie in Walken's lifelong fascination with his own **hair**, which he later admitted was the "secret subtext" to his portrayal of Zorin. "Every time I had a scene with somebody I'd be thinking: 'What do you think of my **hair**? Do you like my hair? Do you like what they did to me? That they made me look like this?' So next time you see the movie, every time I torture somebody I'm really thinking, 'You see what they did to me with this hair?'"

"More. More pow-uh!"

—Max Zorin, exhorting his blimp pilot at the climax of 1985's *A View to a Kill*

VODKA

Walken once described this clear, flavorless spirit as his "**drug** of choice." "Russian vodka, Polish vodka, Czech vodka. I was a vodka expert. It goes right down, but it's not good for you." Sometime in the late 1990s he stopped drinking it entirely. "One day I felt so sick that my wife asked me why I was doing that to myself. I didn't have a good answer, so I stopped. I don't drink hard liquor any more. Long ago I discovered the virtues of great red wine."

VON KARAJAN, HERBERT

Walken once cited this world-renowned Austrian symphony conductor as one of his paragons of manliness. "You go to a symphony, and there are certain conductors who are sexy. Herbert von Karajan is very sexy. It's because you know all the musicians are scared to death of him."

W

WALKEN FOR PRESIDENT

In summer 2005, rumors began to circulate that Walken was planning a presidential run in 2008. A number of websites sprung up promoting his putative candidacy. Several of them even hawked campaign merchandise bearing the "Walken 2008" logo. Sadly, the actor himself had nothing to do with the supposed "grass roots" movement—although he did embrace its underlying principle. "If [the people] want me to be president, I'll do it," Walken told late-night host Conan O'Brien. "What the heck!" Pressed to elaborate on a theoretical Walken presidential platform, he quipped: "No more zoos. . . . I'll let all the animals free."

WALKEN, GEORGIANNE THON

Walken's wife is a former actress and dancer turned big-time Hollywood casting director, whose credits include the HBO hits *Entourage* and *The Sopranos*. The couple first met when they were both appearing in a summertime touring production of *West Side Story* in 1964. Walken was playing Riff, the leader of the Jets, while Georgianne was playing his girlfriend Graziella. "She was a fox," Walken remembers. "She is a fox. We loved each other right away." Georgianne was just as impressed. "When you met him, you knew he had this future," she recalls. "He was good and was gonna be better. . . . I had never met anybody like that in my life." They were married five years later, in 1969.

Early on, Georgianne sacrificed her own career to prop up her new husband's. She sold cosmetics to help make ends meet while Chris was making his bones as a young actor. Even after he hit it big, she largely remained in the background. "My wife takes care of everything for me," Walken once told an interviewer. "She takes care of the bills, money. I don't have any part in it. Everybody has to do something. I do movies, and she takes care of me." By the 1990s,

Georgianne had emerged as a power player in her own right, notching several Emmy awards and numerous nominations for her casting acumen. Of her long union to one of show business's most notorious eccentrics, she once observed: "We've had our ups and downs. We spend a lot of time together and a lot of time apart. That helps."

> *"Chris is ordinary in an unordinary way. He does things to his own timing. Did I tell you that wild animals are attracted to him?"*

—Georgianne Walken, attempting to explain the appeal of her husband

WALKEN, GLENN

Walken's younger brother was the most polished of the acting Walken children. Like **Ronnie**, he started out as a baby model, for the renowned photographer Constance Bannister, and he later moved on to **television**. He got his first call for a commercial try-out when he was five, on TV's *Chance of a Lifetime*. Even at that early age, Glenn seemed to have an uncanny nose for the camera. "He always seemed to know just what to do," the boys' mother **Rosalie Walken** once explained. "Long before the cameraman could tell him what pose to strike, Glenn would seem to sense that in this picture he probably should have his hand in his pocket, or be putting on his gloves, or whatever the case might be." At one point Glenn Walken was on three shows at the same time; when he had a conflict, **Ronnie** would take his place, as they had similar sounding voices.

Asked by a magazine profiler what he wanted to do when he grew up, Glenn replied: "Be an actor and buy a yacht for all the family." Although he never achieved his brother's level of fame, Glenn did forge a respectable acting career of his own—interrupted for a time by a tour of duty in Vietnam. "My younger brother volunteered to go," Christopher said later, "and he went for four years. He was in action in Vietnam. He never talks about it, but I have a feeling he was in rough stuff."

WALKEN, KEN

Walken's older brother Ken was only eight years old when his mother took him from their home in Bayside, Queens into Manhattan to register with the Conover modeling agency. He would blaze a trail for his younger brothers, appearing on Broadway in shows like *The Climate of Eden* and *Anniversary Waltz* and on **television** in *Studio One*, *Kraft Theater*, *Your Show of Shows*, *Mama*, *The Jackie Gleason Show*, and *Treasury Men in Action*. He was also the first of the performing Walkens to capitalize on his **musical** ability. Walken once recalled a memorable example of his brother's ingenuity:

> I remember my older brother went to an audition once. They said, "We're looking for a young man who can play an accordion." My brother raised his hand. He didn't even know what an accordion was. He rented one, had a few lessons, played "Home on the Range," and got the job.

WALKEN, PAUL

Walken's father Paul Walken was a German immigrant who married his mother, Rosalie Russell, in 1936. The son of a baker, Paul Walken spent many years working in bakeries until he saved up enough money to open his own bake shop—Walken's Bakery, located at Broadway and 30th Street in **Astoria**, Queens—where his three sons worked after school.

Ronnie performed some of the more hands-on tasks:

> I used to deliver cakes in a station wagon and work in the back. I was the guy that put the jelly in the doughnuts. In

those days, you'd have a huge can with a plunger on it. It had these two really big needles sticking out each side. You'd take two doughnuts—they'd already be cooked—stick them on those needle things. Then you push the plunger down, and you feel them fill up. There'd usually be a little dribble of jelly on the end. Actually, it was rather sensual.

The family-run bakery business remained in the same location for over sixty years. Paul Walken became a pillar of the community. In the early 1970s, he served as president of the Associated Retail Bakers of Queens. Christopher remembers his father as "a wonderful man . . . very, very hardworking.   But he was also rather spartan in his ways.   I think I inherited some of that.   He was very simple. I mean, I think if he had a billion dollars, he wouldn't live any differently.   He'd eat the same **food** and do the same things." Paul Walken died in 2001.

WALKEN, ROSALIE RUSSELL

Walken's mother emigrated to the United States from Scotland, where she had been a professional dancer. She called herself Roz, after the actress Rosalind Russell and, in Christopher's words, "always had a yen for the theater." "I feel, under different circumstances, my mother could have gone into show business," he said on another occasion. "She was beautiful and she loved being around theater people. She was the one with the wish for me to be an actor, and I'm grateful—it's given me a very interesting life." When Walken was a child, Rosalie joined an organization called the Stage Mothers' Society. She urged him and his brothers to take dancing lessons and enrolled them in Manhattan's Professional Children's School. As the boys began to get bit parts in many of the live television dramas then being produced in New York, Rosalie Walken assumed the role of the benevolent stage mother, ferrying them to and from auditions and kaffee klatsching with the other parents. "There were a lot of these ladies who didn't have to work because their husbands did well," Walken recalls. "They were a tribe unto themselves, these ladies, they were really characters. They had these kids, and they'd take them from show to show. And they all knew each other, and gossiped."

See also **Dancing** and **Women**.

WARHOL, ANDY

The pasty-faced New York art scenester mentions Walken five times in his infamous diaries. In an entry from November 29, 1978, Warhol (*né* Andrew Warhola) mentions a visit to the Coronet Theater in Manhattan for a screening of *The Deer Hunter*, which he refers to as "the new kind of movie—three hours of watching torture." Less than a month later, Warhol recorded a conversation with fellow scenester **Susanna "Tinkerbelle" Campbell** in which she talks about making out with Walken while interviewing him for the February 1979 issue of Warhol's *Interview* magazine. "I guess Tinkerbelle's really wild" is Warhol's characteristically dry summation. On January 12, 1979, the day after he had dinner with comedian Phyllis Diller at New York's La Grenouille restaurant, Warhol has lunch with Tinkerbelle and Walken, who, Warhol reports, "has a moustache now." Walken tells Warhol the story of how he got the name **Christopher** from dancer **Monique Van Vooren**. Four days later, Warhol records that Tinkerbelle has upbraided him for telling people she performed fellatio on Walken. "I told her I didn't tell anybody," Warhol comments, "that I didn't even know." At this point, Walken disappears from Warhol's daily journal, resurfacing only once, in an entry dated March 14, 1985, when Warhol encounters him at a party for producer Dino De Laurentiis at the Alo Alo nightclub in New York. Walken is drunk and has dyed his **hair** blonde—presumably for his role as **Max** Zorin in *A View to a Kill*.

Warhol's high society hanger-on Cornelia Guest recommends a salon where he can go for a touch up, and Walken kisses fellow actor Mickey Rourke on the lips on the way out. "It looked so gay," Warhol concludes.

Walken has refuted or failed to remember the specifics of each of Warhol's diary accounts. ("I'll deny that one absolutely," he remarked of the Tinkerbelle/blowjob story.) Nevertheless, he retained fond memories of the Pittsburgh-born pop art master. "Warhol was famous for being reticent," Walken once observed, "but whenever I was with him we talked about movies, New York, show business. He was very congenial, very intelligent, big mind. He never said anything silly. He said things like 'I believe tomorrow is another day.' Which is silly, except when he said it you could see the mind behind it. I always thought he was rather droll. He was certainly unique."

WAYNE'S WORLD 2   ★★

Walken "parties on" with public access imbeciles Wayne Campbell and Garth Algar in this paint-by-numbers 1993 follow-up to 1992's *Wayne's World*. As Bobby Cahn, a slick record producer who connives to steal Wayne's girlfriend, Walken plays it straight. He was still several years away from developing the comic persona he would deploy in such films as *Joe Dirt*, *The Country Bears*, and *Click*. To be honest, he looks pretty bored throughout. On the plus side, he was in and out of the project in an eye blink. Said Walken: "I've never done a movie that happened so fast." Famed Walken impressionist Kevin Pollak has a cameo as an albino bureaucrat.

"WEAPON OF CHOICE"

"'I think it's going to turn out to be the most popular thing I have ever done," Walken said of this 2001 **music video** from British musician Fatboy Slim. He may be right. The actor won an MTV Video

Music Award for his performance in the video, which paired an irre-sitibily catchy tune with Walken's fleet-footed dancing. Choreographing Walken's moves was Mickey Rooney's son, Michael Rooney. The director was Spike Jonze, best known at the time for the 1999 cult hit *Being John Malkovich*. He approached Walken with his concept for the video after seeing him dance in *Pennies from Heaven*. "I always sort of wanted to film him dancing," Jonze explained. "I just love his face . . . the way it's deadpan. I wrote the treatment around that."

WEDDING CRASHERS WAS A HUGE HIT, BUT WALKEN'S SMALL PART GAVE HIM LITTLE CHANCE TO SHINE.

WEDDING CRASHERS   ★★

Walken's talents are largely wasted in this otherwise amusing comedy about two ne'er-do-wells who invade strangers' wedding receptions as a way to pick up **women**. Vince Vaughn and Owen Wilson are the titular crashers, with Walken relegated to a supporting role as the Secretary of the Treasury. "For me it was something different, to play a father, a good guy," Walken said of his decision to do the film, which became one of the highest-grosing comedies of 2005. "That's the first time I've ever played anybody . . . what can I say? Trustworthy." Unfortunately, while the rest of the film is agreeably ribald, Walken's part is played straight. If you go looking for one of his characteristically over-the-top performances, you're liable to be disappointed.

"When I was a kid, I suppose I crashed some parties. A wedding is different. You have to have the clothes, you have to know some facts in case somebody catches you."

—Walken, on the key to being a successful wedding crasher

WHO AM I THIS TIME?

Walken proves he can adapt his hollow-eyed, intensely moody persona to lighter fare in this 1982 production for PBS' American Playhouse. In a dramatization of Kurt Vonnegut's short story, Walken plays Harry Nash, a shy small-town hardware store clerk who comes to life only when he takes the stage in local "Mask and Wig Club" productions of popular plays like *Cyrano de Bergerac* and *A Streetcar Named Desire*. Susan Sarandon plays a timid bank employee, newly arrived in town, who falls for the introverted amateur thespian. Jonathan Demme directs the charming hour-long drama, which also affords Walken fans a chance to see him overemote in character as Cyrano. "That was the last thing we shot," Walken reported. "They had an auditorium full of local people, in the small town outside of Chicago. They were invited, given sandwiches or something, and we just had the curtain go up, I made my entrance as Cyrano, and I think we shot it in one take. They were like kids in a high school audience, thrilled to be there. It was perfect. I don't know if they would have continued to be that way, but . . . it was sort of like the real thing, like an amateur production of Cyrano."

WILD DUCK, THE

Walken played Gregers Werle in a production of Ibsen's classic play at the Yale Repertory Theater in 1978. It was here that he first developed his distaste for prosthetic enhancements. "The director convinced me that I needed a rubber nose," Walken told the online video podcast *Inner Object*:

> So they had a rubber nose made for me. . . . I put it on and I went onstage and I was completely uncomfortable, so I said to the director: 'I can't do this with a rubber nose.' And he said 'No, it's good, you look uncomfortable.' So I played the part with the rubber nose, I got terrible reviews, and I never did that again.

WILD SIDE   ★★★

Strange as it may seem, *Things To Do in Denver When You're Dead*'s homophobic, wheelchair-bound mob boss was only the second weirdest character Walken played in 1995. The top prize would have to go to Bruno Buckingham, the kinky international money launderer Walken brought to life in this gonzo erotic thriller from British director Donald Cammell. Anne Heche stars as Alex Lee, a high-powered corporate banker who moonlights as a prostitute. She takes Walken as a client, with predictably dangerous consequences. Joan

Chen plays Walken's estranged wife, a **bisexual** footwear magnate who's soon enjoying Heche's sexual favors as well. The impossible-to-follow plot involves a sting operation and the deployment of some kind of computer virus, but exposition is sacrificed in favor of atmospherics, over-the-top acting, and steamy lesbian sex scenes.

Walken has called Bruno Buckingham "the craziest guy I ever played" and it's not hard to see why. Padding around his penthouse apartment in a silk dressing gown and a **black** bob wig, Walken is a visual marvel as he rants about sex, money, and life in prison with a "psycho gorilla" for a cellmate. In one of many bizarre scenes, Walken's character forces a federal agent, played by Steven Bauer, to place a condom on his erect penis before stripping off the agent's briefs, pistol-whipping his bare posterior, and attempting to anally rape him at gunpoint. (For good measure, in an odd bit of product placement, Walken sips Sprite throughout the film.) Even the Man with the Plan looks like a piker compared with this guy.

Is it all worth it? What you think about *Wild Side* depends entirely on what version you see. Producers stripped control of the film from director Donald Cammell and re-edited it without his permission. The resulting truncated version plays like Cinemax-grade softcore. Unfortunately, it's the only version widely circulated in the U.S. The creative dispute may have contributed to Cammell's decision to commit suicide in April 1996. A posthumous "director's cut"—re-edited according to Cammell's specifications—was released in 2000 under the title *Donald Cammell's Wild Side*. Currently available as a European DVD, it's a much better, more coherent film.

"You're here to do Mr. Huge."

—Bruno Buckingham, giving call girl Anne Heche her marching orders,
in 1995's *Wild Side*

WILLY WONKA

Despite never having seen the 1971 original, Walken was considered for the role of the mercurial candymaker in the 2005 remake *Charlie and the Chocolate Factory*. Robin Williams, Nicolas Cage, Steve Martin, and Michael Keaton were also up for the role, which eventually went to Johnny Depp.

WINKLER, HENRY

Walken has called the man who played Fonzie on *Happy Days* "one of the best TV actors I ever saw."

WITNESS IN THE WAR ZONE

See *Deadline*.

WLAKEN

Notoriously misspelled version of Walken's last name that appears in the end credits of Woody Allen's *Annie Hall*. Walken chooses to be amused rather than irritated by the typo. "It's fantastic. Though it's a complete mystery how that happened. Of course, these things are checked and rechecked. It's so carefully looked over that somebody must have really thought that's how my name was spelt. It's very odd."

WOMEN

"Women have always liked me," Walken observed in 1978. "Little ones, tall ones, fat ones, thin ones . . . I think they are attracted by my frivolous nature. And I like playful, intelligent women." He confesses to having a highly competitive nature, but not when it comes to females. "I get jealous of men but never of women. Professionally, I mean. Women are very honest and funny with me. I don't know if they always are with men. With me they use their best jokes." Elsewhere, he has described himself as a "tremendous feminist." "Women have provided the momentum for enormous steps in my life. And I don't know what they think—there's a great mystery involved and maybe that's what I like."

> *"If it were up to me, I'd delegate more responsibility to women. Men's refusal to share the serious tasks with women works to their own detriment. It leaves them with too little time for fishing, playing cards, and drinking wine."*
>
> —Walken, on the battle of the sexes

WONDERFUL JOHN ACTON, THE

In his first recurring television role, Walken played Kevin Acton, the title character's grandson, on this family drama about the life of a county clerk in early twentieth century Kentucky, which ran for several weeks in the summer of 1953.

WOOD, NATALIE

In one of those eerie twists of show business fate, Walken was on board the boat the night this screen idol drowned in the waters near Catalina Island in November 1981. Walken was spending the weekend with Wood and her husband Robert "R. J." Wagner, celebrating the Thanksgiving holiday and the impending completion of their film *Brainstorm*. After a night of drunken revelry, Wood either attempted to leave the boat in a dinghy or tried to stop it from banging against the side of the boat. She slipped and fell overboard and was found dead several hours later. In the aftermath of the tragedy, rumors began to circulate that Walken or Wagner—or perhaps both—might have had something to do with Wood's death. Walken opted not to respond to the speculation. "I just wanted to turn my back on the vulgarity of what was said and printed," he said some years later. "Once, when I read something particularly offensive in a tabloid, I said: 'Okay, that's it. I'm going to find this guy.' So I actually wrote letters and tried to find this guy to look him in the face. But have you ever tried to find someone who writes a scandalous article? I never found the guy because he doesn't exist." He has rarely discussed the Natalie Wood case in interviews—out of respect, he says, for the privacy of her family.

> You know, the curious thing about what happened, while certainly not wishing to diminish it, is that I see things like that every day in the newspaper . . . every day. Somebody fell in their bathtub . . . somebody pulled out of a driveway . . . somebody ate a poisoned Mars Bar. Who the hell knows? But these things happen constantly and I think when it happens to somebody famous it's a different story.

See also **The Mystery of Natalie Wood.**

WORK

Why do you work so much?" is one of the questions that often comes up in Walken interviews—and with good reason. Walken has made more than eighty full-length feature films. Several of those went straight to video. A number of others—like the 2001 comedy *Jungle Juice* starring Robert Wagner and Rutger Hauer—never saw the light of day in any format. Walken himself has admitted there are many films in his oeuvre that even he has never seen. So what lies behind his seeming compulsion to get in front of the camera? It could be as simple as boredom. "I don't have a lot of hobbies," Walken has said. "I don't play golf. I don't have any children. Things that occupy people's time. I just try to take jobs. I basically work so much because I'm lazy." Indeed, other than **cooking** and **painting**, Walken concedes he doesn't really like to do anything besides making movies. "When I don't have any work sometimes, a kind of thing sets in where my mind shuts down. It's almost like hibernation," he says. In these fugue states, he is especially susceptible to saying yes to a lousy script like *Gigli* or *Kangaroo Jack*. Critics may fault him for appearing in a lot of bad movies, but to Walken what's important is that he appear in a lot of movies, period. "I don't choose that much," he says. "I just sort of take what's there."

> *"I really don't have anything else to do."*
>
> —Walken, explaining why he's appeared in over eighty movies

YENTL

Christopher Walken playing the love interest for a cross-dressing Barbra Streisand? It could have happened. Reportedly, Walken was up for the part of Avigdor, the kindly rabbinical student who attracts the affections of Yentl, the Yeshiva Boy, in the 1983 movie **musical** adaptation of Isaac Bashevis Singer's short story. Richard Gere and Michael Douglas had already turned down the chance to serve as Babs's leading mensch, with Kevin Kline also in the running. The part eventually went to Mandy Patinkin, who received a Golden Globe Award nomination for his performance.

YOU ARE THERE

The day is April 18, 1775. Paul Revere is about to set out on his famous ride. And the only man who can stop him is . . . Christopher Walken! In a 1971 episode of this historical reenactment series, Walken dons a powdered wig and a red coat and stakes out Paul Revere's Boston townhouse as a nosy British officer. Wisely, he does not even attempt to do an English accent. Richard Branda plays the midnight rider at the center of the story, with E. G. Marshall as Samuel Adams and future *Tattletales* host Bert Convy as Paul Revere's friend, Dr. Joseph Warren. (Oddly enough, Convy himself had just played Revere a year earlier on an episode of *Bewitched*.) This was one of Walken's rare, periodic forays into costume drama.

ZEN ARCHERY

Walken has likened his approach to acting to Kyudo, the traditional Japanese "way of the bow." In a 1973 interview, Walken explained

> The idea being that when one is a Zen archer, there's a thought and an action, whereas the Western idea tends to be a thought, a decision and an action, and I believe that

acting has a great deal to do with cutting out that middle period. There's something non-verbal about Zen archery: when you pull the arrow back, it goes—and it goes exactly where it's supposed to because you know how to do it. There's no judgment involved.

Walken has called his understanding of zen archery "enormously important in my acting."

ZEN DRIFT

Many people have come up with tongues tied trying to encapsulate Walken's idiosyncratic way of delivering his lines. But the man himself has already put a name to it. "Zen drift" is Walken's term for his customary practice of crossing out most of the **punctuation** in his dialogue, then reading his lines hundreds of times in different voices and dialects until he finds the exact cadence that fits his character.

ZOMBIE MOVIES

"You can never go wrong with a zombie movie," Walken once declared. His love of the living dead genre is well known in Hollywood circles. During a 2003 appearance on *Late Night with Conan O'Brien*, Walken even outlined the plot of a zombie movie in which he wished to star. Entitled *A Zombie Amongst Us*, the proposed film revolved around a group of zombies posing as normal human beings in order to infiltrate the society of the living. Walken envisioned himself playing the hero.

"Zombie movies are interesting because it could be any budget. You can make it for nothing; you can spend a lot of money; it's still a zombie movie."

—Walken, on his love for zombie movies

APPENDIX

WALKENISMS

WORDS OF WISDOM FROM WALKEN ON . . .

ACTING. "A good actor is like a racehorse or a Ferrari. If a cylinder is missing on a Chevy, it doesn't matter that much. But if something's not working right on a Ferrari, it makes a big difference. It's the three percent that makes the difference between good and great."

ADVICE TO FELLOW ACTORS. "When you're in a scene and you don't know what you're gonna do, don't do anything."

CALIFORNIA. "Everything's so mellow out there, you just can't get into a good fight."

CHILDREN. "I don't really enjoy the company of children. When I'm with them I think, gee, I wish this would end so I could have a conversation or something."

CONFRONTATION. "I want conflict in my life. I love arguments with agents, people yelling at me, telling me I'm a jerk. If I can tell someone to drop dead and go to hell, then it's a good day."

DATING. "You don't want to go out with a girl who has a big dog, because when you're together, making it, it will jump all over you."

D.I.Y. "If you want to learn how to build a house, build a house. Don't ask anybody, just build a house."

EDUCATION. "I was never good in school. I didn't like it and always resented having to attend."

GENDER. "I'm glad I'm not a woman for a lot of reasons. Guys have a better deal, that's all there is to it. There's no comparison in terms of anything. Getting a hard-on, that's something a woman will never understand."

HIGH SCHOOL. "I conveniently have no recollection of high school because I would prefer to romanticize my past."

HIS CHOICE OF PROFESSION. "It's very fortunate that I'm an actor. If I worked in an advertising agency or something, I'd probably be fired just for the look in my eye."

HIS HOBBIES. "I stay home a lot. I live in a nice place with trees. I like to stay there."

HIS LOVE OF PRIVACY. "I think I'm better off not socializing. I make a better impression if I'm not around."

HOUSES THAT SMELL. "If a place has a smell, I could not live there."

INTERVIEWS. "I feel about interviews the way I feel about music—that if you take a good piece of music and play it badly it looks like a bad piece of music."

METHOD ACTING. "There's something about the method that I've never understood."

MOVIE TRAILERS. "I don't understand why people pay so much attention to the trailers. I have never known anything about a movie from watching the trailer. It doesn't do anything."

TECHNOLOGY. "I don't own a computer or a mobile phone and I don't even wear a wristwatch. I'm old school."

THERAPY. "I can't understand why actors go to psychiatrists. Who would want to get rid of their problems? Who would want to get better?"

TYPECASTING. "Typecasting is better than no casting."

WHAT TO WEAR. "Black is practical. It always looks clean and fairly neat. It's certainly simple. It's cool. It also makes you look thinner."

WOMEN. "I do like their company very much. I've always gotten along with women very well."

WORK. "I like to work. I mean, what am I going to do? Watch *Court TV* all day?"

WRITING HIS MEMOIRS. "I would write my memoirs, but I can't remember anything."

TALKIN' OF WALKEN

WALKEN'S COLLEAGUES DISH THE DIRT, EXPLAIN THE MYSTIQUE, AND GENERALLY BUTTER HIM UP...

"Nobody else can just sit there and stare at you and give you so many feelings at one time."
—Tim Burton

"You have that sense that there's a hidden agenda. He is saying one thing while something else is going on inside his head—it makes him seem inhabited."
—Paul Schrader

"Chris's special gift as an actor is his willingness to try anything, to constantly explore the possibilities of a scene. He never loses his enthusiasm."
—Michael Cimino

"There's something about him. Sometimes he's very hard to read. He's got such his own style about him. . . . When you watch him it's like watching no one else. He's got a very sharp sense of humor. Everything he did was funny."
—Spike Jonze

"He has some of the best natural instincts of anyone I've worked with. I really think he likes to surprise himself. He comes prepared with some basic ideas of how to play the scene, but after the cameras

are rolling, his instincts kick in."
—Steven Spielberg

"He's got everything: God-given talent, dedication to the work. His mind—he's a brilliant cat. He's got it all going."
—Abel Ferrara

"With Christopher Walken, you never know what you are going to get."
—James Foley, director, *At Close Range*

"Every time Chris Walken says a line, he blows jazz. He comes up with rhythms you never dreamed of and it's just tremendous to watch."
—Hugh Wilson, director, *Blast from the Past*

"His choices are always dangerous, which makes for interesting work. You can watch him eat a bowl of cereal and you'd be riveted because he's just unpredictable."
—Mars Callahan, writer/director, *Poolhall Junkies*

"He's an incredibly withholding character. You look at him, he doesn't jump out at you. You have to come to Chris, and I love that."
—Jordan Roberts, writer/director, *Around the Bend*

"Christopher Walken's a god. Christopher Walken's a genius. Christopher Walken's amazing."
—Nigel Cole, director, *Five Dollars a Day*

"Even when he's being very, very friendly, it's terrifying. Even when he's cracking jokes by the monitors, you feel like he might kill you."
—Ben Garant, writer/director, *Balls of Fury*

"Chris has a way of catching you by surprise and I think he even surprises himself."
—Steven Berkoff, director, *Coriolanus*

"He was very quirky. It was very real, and there's a wonderful warm side to [him]. He's a little bit crazy, but there's a genuine kind of reaching out in that actor."
—Christopher Newton, artistic director, Stratford Shakespeare Festival

"He's a truly gifted comedian. He's just a natural. He speaks in a voice that could only be him. His sense of timing is so unique. So much comedy is about timing, and he's just endlessly surprising."
—Lorne Michaels

"He's a bit intimidating at first glance. Once you get to know him, he's really quite congenial and funny. But he is different. He thinks differently than the rest of us. That uniqueness is why he works so much—you know he's always going to bring something special to the film."
—John Sweet, screenwriter, *The Affair of the Necklace*

"Chris is like a poem. Trying to define him is like trying to define a cloud."
—Sean Penn

"The words don't matter to Chris. He lets them fall where they will. Sometimes it's amazing, and sometimes, honestly, it sucks."
—Dennis Hopper

"There's something about that man. He picks up on cosmic messages, and it's shown through his acting."
—Leonardo DiCaprio

"I'm a huge fan. Chris is unbelievably funny. You either get him or you never get him, and if you don't get him, you go, 'Oh, Chris Walken—isn't he a weirdo?'"
—Rob Lowe

"One of the performances that made me want to be an actor when I was a kid, for some reason, was watching Christopher Walken in *The Deer Hunter*. I don't know what it was about what he did in that movie, but it really resonated in me."
—Oliver Platt

"I think he seems so adorable. I think maybe I was his mom in a past life or something. . . . He's super charming and funny. He touches something in me and I just want to give him a big hug. He's just a big squishy bear."
—Alicia Silverstone

"I think Christopher Walken is the sexiest man alive. He's a babe. Willem Dafoe, too. No offense to these younger actor guys. They don't have that thing yet. A chemical gets released in the lower back that makes the thing. It makes all the difference in the world."
—Christina Applegate

"Every time they were ready to roll the cameras, it didn't matter how many times he did a scene, he did it different."
—Laurence Fishburne

"He's as eccentric and as wacky as you'd expect him to be, but he's also cool."
—Dan Fogler, costar, *Balls of Fury*

"The nicest guy imaginable."
—Sean Patrick Flanery, costar, *Suicide Kings*

"One of the funniest people I've ever met in my life."
—Viggo Mortensen

"Preserved. Taxidermied. Dunked in formaldehyde. Scary."
—Vincent Gallo

"I'm not sure why people are afraid of him. He's a lovely, lovely man."
— Kate Beckinsale

"I remember seeing Christopher Walken in the local grocery shop. He was talking to the vegetables before buying them—that was a bit odd."
—Leonora Reed, marketing executive, 20th Century Fox

"I hope Christopher wins another Oscar. That would be great. I'd like to party with him some time. He's a great dancer."
—Chris Collingwood, songwriter, Fountains of Wayne

"He's a very private person who lives in his head. When that is interrupted, it interferes with his sanity."
—Julian Schnabel

"I was out at some party and I had way too much to drink, and I approached him, to tell him what a big fan I was of his, but in that typical stupid, like drunk guy at 3 am kind of way. And to his credit, he was really gracious, and really nice . . . and very politely walked away."
—Moby

WALKOANS: THE POETRY OF CHRISTOPHER WALKEN

Speaking about Walken, Sean Penn once observed: "Some people got poetry in their blood and some don't. Chris is difficult to track. It's hard to figure out whether it's angelic or satanic. But it certainly is poetic." Apropos of that insight, here are some real quotes from Christopher Walken, reconfigured as Zen poems.

On *The Deer Hunter*
It was a wonderful movie
Very popular
Many people saw it
Oscar

The Prison of Self
One day I was sitting in my dressing room
Reading a book, just killing time
When I quickly glanced at myself in the mirror
And almost as quickly, I looked away
As if I didn't want to see that person
I remember thinking to myself:
"I hope he leaves . . . without saying goodbye."

For John Turturro, On the Occasion of *Romance & Cigarettes'* **Impending Release**
I haven't seen it

It's coming
It's a musical
Susan Sarandon, James Gandolfini, Steve Buscemi

To a Child Who Has Found His Muse
Whenever I can
I like to look at kids' paintings
It's almost as if you cannot find a bad one
It's always interesting
Why is that?

On Being Called Creepy
I hope I'm not creepy
Creepy is not a mammal
Creepy is like an insect
Spooky is OK
Racehorses get spooked, they're emotional

The Good Actor Eschews Research
Information
Almost you could say
Confuses me
I just make it up

The Art of the Schmear
Big, splash, colorful
Like flowers, my paintings are like flowers
I have a whole bunch of them
They're sort of cheery

A Christmas Memory

Nobody is scared of me
I dressed up as Santa Claus once
Well, that's bound to be pretty scary

Malediction on Malta, 2002

I hardly ever go in the sun
I don't like it because it hurts
It hurts your eyes

Ode to DeCecco

At one point I had a pasta machine
I tried that
They make it look easy
But it's not
Making your own pasta is not easy

Thoughts on Free Will

People talk to me about my choices
I don't make choices, hardly
Things happen, and you say yes or no
What's the choice?

Memories of Childhood

When I was a kid
I'd pass out sometimes
Because I'd get real slow
The blood, you know
But when you get older, that's good

BIBLIOGRAPHY

Periodicals

Aames, Ethan. "Interview: Christopher Walken on *Around the Bend*." *Cinema Confidential*. October 5, 2004.

Baird, Kirk. "King for a Day." *Las Vegas Sun*. June 15, 2005.

Buckalew, Brett. "Leaving the Villains Behind." Filmstew.com. October 13, 2004.

Canby, Vincent. "Walken Conjures up the King." *New York Times*. January 6, 1995.

Chambers, Andrea. "From Any Distance, At Close Range Star Christopher Walken Comes Off As Edgy, Electric And Elusive." *People*. April 27, 1986.

"Christopher Walken on Being Prez: 'What the Heck!'" Spin.com. September 29, 2006.

Corsello, Andrew. "Christopher Walken Must Die." *Gentlemen's Quarterly*. March 2000.

Dargis, Manohla "Learning to Be Fathers and Learning to Be Sons." *New York Times*. October 8, 2004.

Feingold, Michael. "Gull Talk." *Village Voice*. August 15-21, 2001.

Flatley, Guy. "Walken Tall with Chris." *Cosmopolitan*. January 1981.

Gilchrist, Todd. "Around the Bend: An Interview with Christopher Walken." Blackfilm.com. October 2004.

Gostin, Nicki. "Christopher Walken." *Newsweek*. July 3, 2006.

Grobel, Lawrence. "Walken Tall." *Hollywood Life*. May 2004.

Gussow, Mel. "Theater: Camus's 'Caligula' Is Staged." *New York Times*. December 10, 1971.

Gussow, Mel. "Theater: 'Hamlet,' with Walken, in Connecticut." *New York Times*. August 23, 1982.

Haller, Scot. "I Am the Malevolent WASP." *Esquire*. January 1981.

Hedegaard, Erik. "The Devil Inside." *Details*. December 1993.

Helman, Marian. "Three Young Musketeers." *TV Radio Mirror*. April 1956.

Kahn, Joseph P. "More Cowbell? Yes, Please, We've Got a Fever." *Boston Globe*. April 30. 2005.

Kerr, Walter. "This Emperor Is Something to See." *New York Times*. December 12, 1971.

Kirschling, Gregory. "Walken 'Around.'" *Entertainment Weekly*. October 22, 2004.

Kuntz, Tom. "Top Hat And One Weird Cat." *New York Times*. September 2, 2001.

Lemons, Stephen. "Christopher Walken." Salon.com. October 10, 2000.

Martinez, Michael. "Cookin' with Christopher Walken." *Shout Magazine*. August, 2001.

Maslin, Janet. "After Decades in a Bomb Shelter, a Family Learns the Only Fallout Is Social." *New York Times*. February 12, 1999.

McLellan, Jim. "Interview: Christopher Walken." *The Face*. June 1994.

Mitchell, Elvis. "No More Mr. Regular Citizen: It's Back to the Bad Old Days." *New York Times*. August 11, 2000.

Nashawaty, Chris. "The Greats: Christopher Walken." *Entertainment Weekly*. March 17, 2000.

Nelson, Arty. "The Chris Walken Song and Dance: A Serious Story." *Bikini*. July 1995.

Norman, Neil. "Walken Talks." *The Face*. February 1985.

Pearlman, Cindy. "Actor Enjoys Stepping Outside Evil Persona." *Columbus Dispatch*. June 23, 2006.

Pearlman, Sandy. "A Christopher Walken Moment." *Chicago Sun-Times*. October 14, 2003.

"Playboy Interview: Christopher Walken." *Playboy*. September 1997.

Ralstob, Gary. "My Heart Belongs Only to Glasgow." *Daily Record*. October 24, 2001.

Richter, Erin. "Walken After Midnight." *Entertainment Weekly*. June 16, 1995.

Rodrick, Stephen. "Odd Man In." *New York Times Magazine*. May 30, 2004.

Rose, Tiffany. "Interrogation: Christopher Walken." *UK Sunday Mirror*. July 15, 2007.

Rose, Tiffany. "It's Just Too Good to Be True for Walken." *New Zealand Herald*. August 6, 2005.

Saban, Stephen. "Walken After Midnight." *Esquire*. December 1995.

Scherzer, Barbara. "Walken's Name on Marquee." *Daily Variety*. June 16, 2005.

Scott, A. O. "Men Navigating Subplots While Shooting Pool." *New York Times*. February 28, 2003.

Scott, A.O. "Seeking Glory, and Fighting Evil, with a Paddle." *New York Times*. August 29, 2007.

Smith, Gavin. "Out There on a Visit." *Film Comment*. July/August 1992.

Stacy, Greg. "More Cowbell!" *OC Weekly*. June 22, 2006.

Steinbruner, Greg. "Walken the Mild Side." *New Jersey Star-Ledger*. June 13, 2004.

Stoop, Norma McClain. "All I Want to Do Is Feel the Warmth." *After Dark*. May 1973.

Terry, Wallace. "It's Hard For Me to Play the Guy Next Door." *Parade*. September 21, 1997.

Tinkerbelle. "Off the Wall with Walken." *Interview*. August 1977.

Vinch, Chuck. "Wedding Wackiness." *Air Force Times*. August 1, 2005.

Vrabel, Jeff. "Christopher Walken: An Appreciation." *Chicago Sun-Times*. April 25, 2004.

Walcott, James. "Walken on the Wild Side." *New Yorker*. January 9, 1995.

"Walken Marries Travolta." *Time Out London*. August 17, 2001.

"Walken Struts Stuff in Video." *Chicago Sun-Times*. March 24, 2001.

Wartofsky, Alona. "The Walken Shtick, Creepy . . . and Cool." *Washington Post*. August 5, 2001.

Weinraub, Bernard. "At Lunch with: Christopher Walken." *New York Times*. June 24, 1992.

"What Walken Watches." *FilmStew*. June 19, 2007.

Books
Bach, Steven. *Final Cut: Art, Money, and Ego in the Making of* Heaven's Gate*, the Film That Sank United Artists*. New York: William Morrow & Co, 1985.

Bjorkman, Stig. *Woody Allen on Woody Allen*. New York: Grove Press, 1993.

Chubbuck, Ivana. *The Power of the Actor*. New York: Gotham, 2004.

Duno, Steve. *K.I.S.S. Guide to Cat Care*. New York: Dorling Kindersley, 2001.

Harris, Warren G. *Natalie & R. J.* New York: Doubleday, 1988.

Hunter, Jack. *Christopher Walken: Movie Top Ten*. Washington, D.C.: Creation Books, 2000.

Lambert, Gavin. *Natalie Wood: A Life*. New York: Back Stage Books, 2005.

Lowenstein, Stephen. *My First Movie*. New York: Penguin, 2002.

1990 Current Biography Yearbook. Bronx, NY: H. W. Wilson Co., 1990.

Shales, Tom and James Andrew Miller. *Live from New York*. New York: Little Brown and Company, 2002.

Shewey, Don. *Caught in the Act: New York Actors Face to Face*. New York: New American Library, 1986.

Warhol, Andy and Pat Hackett. *The Andy Warhol Diaries*. New York: Grand Central Publishing, 1991.

INDEX

ACKNOWLEDGEMENTS

I'd like to thank the following people for their help in researching this book: Jane Klain and the staff of the Paley Center for Media, Joanna Ney (Film Society of Lincoln Center), Aubrey T. Dancy, Kathleen Hagiwara, Janine Lehmann, and John Lazarus.